Guide to the Appalachian Trail in Maine

Thirteenth Edition
1996

Maine Appalachian Trail Club, Inc.
Box 283, Augusta, Maine 04332

Guide Editors Dean Cilley · Susan Cilley

Overseers of the Trail Priscilla Seimer · Bob Cummings · Chris Wolfe · Patrick Will · John Morgan

Contributors Include
Topographic Maps: Clarence R. "Charlie" Gilman ·
Guidebook: Stephen Clark · Ned Claxton, M.D. · Chris Dorion · David Field · David Forrant · Harold Hanson · Paul P. Johnson, Jr. · Lester Kenway · Jeff Ryan · Elsa Sanborn

Special thanks to William Hancock, Erik Hargreaves, Judy Hays, Chris Mathan, John Wainer

Guidebook Design Bruce Kennett

Cover Photograph *Katahdin from the West Branch of the Penobscot River.* Photograph ©1996 by Jeffrey Stevensen.

Printing History

1st Edition	1934	6th Edition	1964	11th Edition	1988
2nd Edition	1936	7th Edition	1969	2nd printing	1990
3rd Edition	1938	8th Edition	1975	12th Edition	1993
4th Edition	1942	9th Edition	1978	13th Edition	1996
5th Edition	1953	10th Edition	1983		

Published by the Maine Appalachian Trail Club, Inc.
P.O. Box 283, Augusta, Maine 04332-0283
in cooperation with The Appalachian Trail Conference,
P.O. Box 807, Harpers Ferry, West Virginia 25425

Thirteenth Edition. Printed in the United States of America.

ISBN 0–917953–90–8

Printed on recycled paper.

Notice to Trail Users

The information contained in this guide reflects the work of many volunteers. The editors have made their best efforts to ensure that the information gathered is accurate at the time of publication. Natural changes occur constantly along the trail and make relocations and maintenance efforts necessary. Information regarding trail access may continue to change due to logging or other developments near the Trail corridor. Use of information in this guide is at the sole risk of the user.

Enjoy your hike, but take all appropriate precautions for your safety and well-being.

Purify drinking water drawn from any source. The Appalachian Trail Conference and the Maine Appalachian Trail Club attempt to identify sources of water along the Trail. They have no control over these sources and cannot, in any sense, be responsible for the availability or quality of the water at any given time. The purity of water from natural sources found along the Trail cannot be guaranteed. All water should be treated before use.

Certain risks are inherent in any Appalachian Trail hike. Each A.T. user must accept personal responsibility for his or her safety while on the Trail. The Appalachian Trail Conference and the Maine Appalachian Trail Club cannot ensure the safety of any hiker on the Trail. When undertaking a hike on the Trail, each user thereby assumes the risk for any accident, illness, or injury that might occur.

APPLICATION FOR MEMBERSHIP
(Please photocopy this page)

We invite you to join the MAINE APPALACHIAN TRAIL CLUB. Your membership and support of this volunteer organization enables the MATC to maintain a high quality hiking trail through the Maine woods. Your membership includes five copies annually of the **MAINEtainer**, the club newsletter.

Please send the membership form and check to:

MAINE APPALACHIAN TRAIL CLUB
P.O. BOX 283
AUGUSTA, ME 04332-0283

For Individual Membership ($10.00) _____

Family Membership ($15.00) _____

Organizational Membership ($20.00) _____

Life Membership ($250.00) _____

Contribution _____

NAME _____

ADDRESS _____

TOWN _____ STATE _____ ZIP _____

List family members who wish to receive membership cards:

TO THOSE who would see the Maine wilderness, tramp day by day through a succession of ever delightful forest, past lake and stream, and over mountains, we would say: Follow the Appalachian Trail across Maine. It cannot be followed on horse or awheel. Remote for detachment, narrow for chosen company, winding for leisure, lonely for contemplation, it beckons not merely north and south but upward to the body, mind and soul of man.

— Myron H. Avery, *In the Maine Woods* (1934)

Table of Contents

The Appalachian Trail
in Maine

Detail
on Map 4

● Bangor

Detail
on Map 6

Portland
●

1

General Information

FORMAT OF THIS GUIDE

This guide consists of two linked components, a guidebook and a series of seven map sheets. The book contains general orientation and trip planning information, and provides supplementary information on "points of interest" along the Trail. On one side of each map sheet is a topographic map showing the alignment of the Trail and a profile diagram showing the vertical relief of the Trail. On the reverse side of each map sheet is specific Trail data and mileages, information about lean-tos and campsites, and descriptions for road access and side trails. A general access map for the area south of the Kennebec River is provided on Map 6; a similar map for most of the area north of the Kennebec is on Map 4.

The guide is arranged to provide general background information regarding the Trail and what to expect, suggestions for hikes of various lengths and difficulty, a description of plants and animals found along the Trail, and the history and management of the Trail as a whole and in Maine in particular. Chapter 6, Trail Synopsis by Map, includes a comprehensive overview for each section of trail, including a "points of interest" section for each map, to provide the interested hiker with more background information about the area being traversed. Where possible, details have been arranged in table format for easy reference.

In an effort to organize trail access information, the Trail descriptions and the north and southbound mileages are divided into thirteen sections beginning at Katahdin and progressing south. Divisions of sections occur at a significant geographical feature or road crossing. Because sections may be of different lengths, each map may contain a different number of sections.

Trail descriptions and mileages run in columns on the map sheets. Each column includes a diagram which is a visual representation of the Trail, drawn to align with the Trail descriptions for easy cross-reference. Lean-tos, campsites, and distances between them are clearly marked. These diagrams are not drawn to scale or with true reference to compass direction and should not be used for technical navigation.

User input is welcome. All suggestions should be addressed to: Guide Editor, MATC, P.O. Box 283, Augusta, ME 04332-0283.

ROUTE OF THE APPALACHIAN TRAIL IN MAINE

The northern terminus of the Appalachian Trail is the summit of Katahdin (Baxter Peak, elevation 5,267 ft.). From Baxter State Park, northwest of the town of Millinocket, the Trail trends in a general southwesterly direction across the state, 281 miles to the Maine–New Hampshire state line, northwest of the town of Bethel.

Geographically, the Trail can be divided into three major regions: the northern, from Katahdin to Monson, a distance of 114 miles; the central, from Monson to Long Falls Dam Road near the east end of Bigelow Mountain, a distance of 54 miles; and the southern, from Long Falls Dam Road to the Maine –New Hampshire state line northwest of the village of Bethel, a distance of 113 miles.

The northern region includes a multitude of wild lakes and ponds, several peaks (including Katahdin, the White Cap range, and the Barren–Chairback range), and the watersheds of the West Branch of the Penobscot River and the Pleasant River. This northern area offers substantial logistical problems to the hiker as it traverses relatively unbroken timberlands in the largest forested area on the East Coast. The northern region of the A.T. in Maine is covered by Maps 1, 2, and 3.

The central region is the easiest from a hiker's standpoint.

There are only two low mountains to traverse, Moxie Bald Mountain, and Pleasant Pond Mountain. A long stream walk along the West Branch of the Piscataquis River, the ferry crossing of the Kennebec River, and a passage through the historic Carry Ponds area are features of this region. The central area of the A.T. in Maine is covered by Map 4 and Section 6 of Map 5.

The spectacular southern region is the most difficult due to the numerous high peaks encountered. The Trail crosses seven 4,000 foot peaks (two others are on short side trails) and thirteen other peaks above 3,000 feet. Considerable gain and loss of elevation often occurs between these summits. Some of the major mountains include: Bigelow, Sugarloaf, Saddleback, Old Blue, Baldpate, and the peaks of the Mahoosuc range. This mountainous portion is covered by Section 7 of Map 5 and all of Maps 6 and 7.

TRAIL MARKING

The primary method for marking the Appalachian Trail is a 2 inch by 6 inch rectangular blaze of white paint placed at eye level. Trail blazes are generally placed on trees that are most likely to catch the hiker's eye. Where there are no trees convenient to the trail, the white paint blaze may be on a prominent rock or post. The nature of the trail determines how close together blazes are located. The general goal is to be able to see from one blaze to the next. Areas of the trail that require the hiker's special attention, such as obscure areas, a change in the trail direction, or a trail junction, may be marked with double blazes (one directly over the other). Side trails are similarly marked using blue paint blazes.

Directional signs, located at trailheads, junctions, or other important points along the Trail, give distances to destinations such as lean-tos, road crossings or prominent features along the trail. The Maine Appalachian Trail Club maintains about 400 of these traditional brown "rustic" wooden signs. Educational information and regulatory signs may be posted at campsites, shelters, or trailheads along the A.T.

GENERAL INFORMATION

The mileages noted in the trail descriptions have been derived by measuring the trail with a professional surveyor's wheel. It is possible that trail description mileages differ from mileages posted on signs. At the time of publication of this guide (1996), the trail description mileage is likely to be the more accurate. MATC volunteers carry out a regular program of sign maintenance and replacement. Please do not remove or deface signs.

Cairns — carefully placed piles of rock usually from 2 to 5 feet high — mark the trail above timberline or in barren areas. Cairns are particularly helpful in locating the route in fog.

TRAIL USE AND PRECAUTIONS

The information contained in this guide reflects the work of many volunteers. The editors have made their best efforts to ensure that the information gathered is accurate at the time of publication. Natural changes occur constantly along the Trail and make relocations and maintenance efforts necessary. Please remember, no published route information is going to be 100% accurate at the time you read it. Significant relocations or changed trail routes will be indicated by trail signs and information posted at lean-tos. Information about recent changes can be obtained before your hike by writing to: The Maine Appalachian Trail Club, P.O. Box 283, Augusta, ME 04332-0283.

Staying on the Trail

Since some sections of the Trail in Maine are relatively remote, it is important to remember these essential precautions:

In case of doubt as to the route, stop. Do not go forward. Insistence on going forward when the route seems obscure or dubious is a cardinal mistake. Retrace your route deliberately, slowly, and carefully until you find the last white blaze which served as a clear indication of the Trail.

Know how to use a map and a compass, and carry them with you. Use the map to follow your progress as you hike. The trail descriptions on the reverse of the map often clarify the general direction of travel by using compass directions (NE, SW, etc.).

Side Trails

The MATC maintains the blue-blazed side trails to the same standards as the Appalachian Trail. Some of the side trails receive far less use than the A.T. and do not have the well-worn footbed typically found on most sections of the Trail.

Register Boxes

The MATC maintains several register boxes along the A.T. Information gathered at these register boxes is used by the MATC for both planning and maintenance purposes. Help us do a better job of managing the Trail by completing a card at each box you pass.

Season for Travel

The season for A.T. travel in Maine is comparatively short, extending from late May to early November. At lower elevations, mid-summer temperatures average seventy to eighty degrees Fahrenheit during the day and drop to the low sixties at night. From August through early November, cooler temperatures prevail, making it a popular time to hike in Maine.

Summer weather can be changeable and the Trail in Maine is justly famed for its rain! Dampness is a problem, especially for hiking boots. Apply a waterproof treatment to your footwear to minimize water damage.

Carry sufficient clothing to provide protection from wind and wet. Even in the summer months, there is a real danger of hypothermia — particularly at higher elevations or in wet conditions. Keep an eye on the weather; high winds, fog, and chilling rain are potential killers.

Black flies, mosquitoes, and midges (no-see-ums), which are prevalent in the Maine woods from May through July, have generally disappeared by the middle of August. Hikers who have never experienced the dense clouds of frenzied black flies in June should be forewarned that these annoying insects make living in the out-of-doors seriously challenging during this period. Wet or rainy weather may prolong the black fly season. Midge-proof tents with no-see-um netting are essential for a good night's sleep. There are several good insect repellents on the market, but in periods of heavy fly hatches, even very good repellents will merely dampen the bugs' ardor.

The Appalachian Trail in Maine is neither designed nor maintained for winter travel. The harshness of common winter conditions requires an explicit warning. Deep snow and winter conditions can be expected anytime on the Trail in Maine from October to May. Knowledge of weather conditions is critical during this period. Sudden deep snows accompanied by strong winds can quickly create life-threatening situations.

During the winter, a snow depth of three to five feet is normal and eight feet or more is not uncommon. Trail markings, and even lean-tos, may be completely covered by snow, and safe stream crossings may become impossible. Even as late as Memorial Day, deep snow may be found in the higher elevations, particularly in western or northern Maine. These conditions present a serious danger to hikers who are not experienced and equipped with snowshoes or skis, an ice axe and crampons.

Hiking the A.T. during the spring can be difficult and unpleasant. Deep snowdrifts may obscure the Trail and make hiking exhausting. Cold streams swollen with snow-melt or spring rains may be difficult or impossible to cross safely. Hikers should not underestimate the difficulty of travel in such conditions. In addition to the problems presented by snow, hiking on the Trail while the ground is thawing severely damages the Trail itself.

Hunting Season

The National Park Service (NPS) owns much of the land along the Appalachian Trail. Federal regulations prohibit hunting and trapping on these lands. However, some of the boundary lines that identify these lands have yet to be surveyed. It may be difficult for hunters to know when they are on National Park Service lands.

Except for Baxter State Park, hunting is permitted along the A.T. on both private lands and on state-owned lands other than those of the Bureau of Parks and Lands (BP&L). State regulations prohibit hunting along the Trail and within 300 feet of the Trail where it crosses BP&L property. However, on both NPS and BP&L lands, hunters who approach the Appalachian Trail from the side, and do not know they are on Trail lands, may have no idea that the Trail is nearby.

Because of this situation, *the Maine Appalachian Trail Club strongly advises hikers and other users of the Appalachian Trail to wear fluorescent orange during the hunting seasons.* The primary hunting seasons run from September through November, depending on the game species. All hunting is prohibited on Sundays. It is illegal to interfere with lawful hunting activities.

If you encounter a dangerous situation because of hunting in the Appalachian Trail Corridor, please send a detailed account to: MATC, P.O. Box 283, Augusta, ME 04332-0283.

Fire Danger

All travelers in the Maine woods should exercise extreme care to avoid fire danger. A fire caused by an A.T. hiker would have a disastrous effect since the Trail is only a narrow corridor through privately owned forest. Campfires are allowed only in the fireplace at the designated lean-tos and campsites along the Trail. Smokers should stop to smoke, carefully extinguish all embers, and carry out cigarette butts.

Anyone who leaves a fire unattended which gets out of control and causes damage is legally responsible for all the costs of fire suppression and property damage (including timber value). Be sure your fire is "dead out" when you leave it.

Lightning

Lightning is the tremendous discharge of electricity that builds up in cumulo-nimbus clouds (thunderheads). Discharges may be from ground to cloud, cloud to cloud, or cloud to ground. While it is unusual to be struck by lightning, such a strike can easily be fatal.

Lightning tends to strike objects that stick up above their surroundings either on land or in water. A lightning strike spreads in all directions as it dissipates into the ground. For that reason, avoid tall trees, hilltops, open summits, or tall structures such as power line towers or fire towers. Do not make yourself the tallest thing around — and do not take shelter near the tallest thing around. A tent offers no protection from lightning. Get off peaks or cliffs, and stay away from high points and the ends of ridges. Find shelter in lower clumps of shorter trees. Stay away from water. If you are in the water, get out. If caught in the open, crouch down on your feet, keeping them close together. Keep your hands off the ground, and do not lie down. If possible, use dry insulation such as a foam pad between yourself and the ground. Avoid being near metal objects such as metal pack frames, tent poles, knives, or fishing gear. If you are with a group, spread out to minimize the likelihood of several people being struck by lightning.

Animals

Poisonous snakes are not common at the elevation and latitude of the Appalachian Trail in Maine.

Rodents including porcupines, mice, chipmunks and squirrels are common, particularly around shelters. They can be very destructive to shelters, privies, and personal equipment (including packs and boots) when in search of food. While black bears are common in the Maine woods, they have not been a problem at campsites and shelters.

To help discourage animal visitors, it is a good idea to hang food well out of reach. Keeping a clean camp will help prevent problems for you and for others who follow.

Beaver dams sometimes create flowages which flood and obliterate the trail for some distance. Watch for blazes as you carefully skirt around the flowage to rejoin the Trail.

Pack animals are not allowed on the A.T.

Dogs can be a nuisance or threat to other hikers and chase

the wildlife found along the Trail. Chasing wildlife can be life threatening to the chased as well as dangerous to the dog (particularly when porcupines are involved). The territorial instincts of dogs often result in fights with other dogs. If a pet cannot be strictly controlled, it should be left home. In addition, many at-home pets' muscles, foot pads, and sleeping habits are not adaptable to the rigors of A.T. hiking.

Compass Declination

The compass declination in Maine is approximately 18 degrees west. This means that true north (map north) is 18 degrees clockwise from the compass needle. This is considerable variation and should be taken into account. This variation, also known as magnetic declination, is shown on each map included with this Guide.

Group Hikes and Special Events

Special events, group hikes, or other group activities that could degrade the Appalachian Trail's natural or cultural resources or social values should be avoided. Examples of such activities include publicized spectator events, commercial or competitive activities, or programs involving large groups.

Other Information Sources

Developments and matters of interest along the entire Appalachian Trail are reported in the *Appalachian Trailway News*, (published five times annually by the Appalachian Trail Conference). While it is not intended as a guidebook supplement, it does include maps and details of relocations and other significant changes. It also includes interesting articles about trail activities and management issues.

The Appalachian Trail Conference also produces other publications for hikers. *The Appalachian Trail Thru-hikers' Companion* is particularly useful to long-distance hikers needing additional information about services near the Trail. It is updated on an annual basis and includes detailed information about the entire Trail.

The *Maine Atlas and Gazetteer* published by DeLorme Publishing Company in Freeport, Maine, is an indispensable aid to navigating the back roads of Maine.

TRAIL ETHICS

When hikers were few and far between, trail etiquette was a subject hardly worth discussing. People were so glad to see each other along the trail that they treated each other like long lost friends. Today, with the increased popularity of hiking, it is not unusual to share the trail and campsites with dozens of fellow hikers. Common sense and respect for others should be the rule whenever people are grouped together.

Trail etiquette includes hiking without leaving a trace of your passage. Hiking "without a trace" means:

respecting the environment by
- protecting the delicate ecosystems of the higher elevations
- leaving ground cover in place
- leaving all living plants unharmed
- carrying a portable stove for cooking
- camping or building fires only in designated places
- never building a fire above treeline
- using only dead wood
- making sure your fire is completely out
- walking on rocks above treeline and not on the fragile alpine plants

respecting others who are using the Trail by
- washing away from the water supply, not in it
- using the provided toilet facilities
- carrying out what is carried in
- welcoming others and sharing facilites with them
- limiting a stay to two nights at a shelter
- leaving a site better than it was on arrival
- providing one qualified leader for each four youths
- limiting the size of a group to ten persons

respecting your own needs and abilities by
- planning a trip carefully within your limitations
- informing family and friends of your plans
- carrying adequate food, clothing and equipment
- taking time to enjoy the surroundings
- keeping each wilderness experience as natural and meaningful as possible.

When hikers agree to rules of conduct that minimize their impact on the trail and fellow hikers' trail experience, then we are truly hiking "without a trace".

PERSONAL SAFETY

The Appalachian Trail Conference makes the following suggestions for hiker security on the Trail:

- Don't hike alone. A partner reduces the potential for harassment. If you do hike alone, say you are with a larger group.
- Leave your trip itinerary and timetable with family or friends. If you use a "Trail name" be sure your home contacts know the name.
- Don't broadcast your itinerary to strangers or leave it on your vehicle. Do not describe the whereabouts of fellow hikers.
- Avoid provocation.
- Be cautious with strangers.
- Camp away from roads. Harassment is most likely in areas accessible to motor vehicles.
- Don't carry firearms.
- Discourage theft. Don't leave your pack unattended. Don't leave cash, cameras, or expensive camping equipment in cars parked at trailheads.
- If you witness harassment or become a victim, promptly report the incident to local law enforcement authorities, the State Police, and the ATC so that steps can be taken to prevent recurrence.

The ATC, in cooperation with the MATC, is developing a more formal emergency information network. When complete, it will include posting emergency information at shelters and other key points along the Trail. In the meantime, use common sense, be prudent, and be cautious.

WATER AND SANITATION

Water quality cannot be taken for granted. A water source may be free running, look clear, smell appetizing, and taste good. Although you may see wildlife drinking from it, hikers cannot assume that any water is safe to drink without purification.

A microscopic protozoan known as *Giardia lamblia*, is one of several disease-causing organisms that may be present in "clean" looking water. The Giardia organism is spread by fecal contamination of the water supply. The disease Giardiasis (pronounced gee-ar-dye-a-sis), sometimes known as "Beaver Fever", has many other carriers including dogs and people.

The Maine Appalachian Trail Club (MATC) makes no guarantee as to the safety or availability of any water along the Trail. No source of water can be trusted to be safe for consumption without treatment. Treatment alternatives include boiling, mechanical filtration or chemical treatment. You are responsible for treating all water you consume.

Lean-tos and campsites along the Appalachian Trail in Maine have privies nearby. Along the Trail itself, take care in the choice of sites for eliminating body wastes. Stay at least 200 feet downhill away from any water source or drainage. Bury wastes in four to six inches of soil, as this depth best promotes decomposition.

Use "biodegradable" soap, and wash your dishes and yourself away from any water source. Dispose of waste water away from drinking water and in accordance with the locations suggested above. Never put food particles or any other wastes into any water supply.

TRIP PLANNING

Proper trip planning can make the difference between a safe, enjoyable hike and a miserable or even dangerous experience. Proper trip planning includes matching the difficulty of the terrain to the capabilities of trip participants, matching the length of the trip (including travel time to and from the Trail) to the time available for the trip, and ensuring that participants' needs for food, shelter, and clothing have all been provided for.

Obtain an understanding of the area you intend to visit. Study the guidebook and maps to develop your familiarity with the terrain and landmarks. If you need to, write for further local information. Talk with others who have done the same or a similar trip. Become familiar with the prevailing weather for the area.

Understand your skills and physical limits and those of your companions. If young children are part of your group, you should plan to do a trip of different length and difficulty than if the party consists solely of strong, experienced adult hikers. Besides the obvious difference in physical size and strength, young children are not goal-oriented the way adults are. If you are in good shape, you can manage more ambitious trips with less fatigue. Fatigue lessens a hiker's margin of safety. Inexperienced hikers should consider beginning with shorter or weekend trips. Find more experienced hikers to travel with, and learn from their experience. Learn how much you can comfortably carry, how to load your pack, and how to listen to your body. Learn about safe travel in the mountains, techniques for stream crossings, and the danger of lightning on open ridges during thunderstorms. Understand first aid and the threat of hypothermia.

Being properly equipped is the final aspect of trip planning. Evaluate your anticipated needs based upon the variety of situations you will be likely to encounter. These will change depending on the length of your trip, the elevation of the trip, the weather and season of the year, and the abilities of others in your party. Try out clothing and equipment in non-critical situations before equipment deficiencies or failure put you in a difficult situation. Think ahead — carry a repair kit. Replace old equipment when its useful lifetime is nearing the end, don't wait for catastrophic failure.

The adventure on the Trail is in the unknown and the unexpected. Proper trip planning provides the margin of safety that lets you meet the challenges and enjoy your outdoor experience.

HIKING EQUIPMENT

Gear and Clothing

Whether you are hitting the trail for an afternoon or for six months, proper gear and clothing are necessary for a safe and comfortable hike. When purchasing equipment, keep two things in mind: the quality of the equipment and its weight. Quality equipment can make the difference between an enjoyable hike and a miserable one. If you are caught in a bad storm, you will be glad you spent every cent on shelter that keeps you warm and dry. Don't carry more equipment than you need. You can't have a pleasurable hike if you are overburdened. Pack enough gear to provide a margin of safety for the unexpected, but don't overdo it. Pack the lightest equipment you can find that will stand up to rugged use. Many gadgets look good on the store shelf, but ask yourself if they will be truly useful in the back country. When you are loading your pack, "take care of the ounces and the pounds will take care of themselves."

Equipment Checklist

The following items should be included for day trips or longer excursions and will add to your enjoyment of the Appalachian Trail:

> **Wear:**
> Hiking shoes
> Socks (for comfort and cushioning)
> Pants and shirt (suitable for variable weather conditions)
> Wool hat or sun hat

Hiking Equipment

Top or outside pockets of your pack:
Guidebook
Map and compass
Handkerchief or bandanna
Matches in waterproof case
Pocket knife
Flashlight or headlamp (with spare batteries and bulb)
Toilet paper
Insect repellent
Water bottles or canteens
Notebook and pencil
Extra socks
Jacket or windbreaker
Raingear
First aid kit (include Moleskin®)
Extra food
Sun protection (sunglasses, sunscreen, lip balm)
Whistle
A handful of sealable plastic bags
Camera and film (optional)
Binoculars (optional)

For overnight trips, carry inside your pack:
Sleeping bag
Lightweight mattress (ground pad)
Toilet articles
Plastic bag with extra:
    shirt and pants, handkerchiefs, underwear
Plastic litter bag
Food
Eating utensils
Repair kit
Cooking equipment
Dishwashing gear
Portable stove and fuel
Tent

Footwear

The Appalachian Trail in Maine is rugged and damp. Sturdy boots are essential for protection and support, regardless of length of hike. Hiking boots generally fall into three categories: Day Hikers, for hikes of less than one day's duration; Weekend Boots, for hikes of 2–3 days; and Backpacking Boots, for extended hikes.

Day Hikers are made with fabric and leather uppers. They are lightweight and comfortable for short hikes and casual wear, but are not designed for the extended punishment of daily trail life.

Weekend Boots are also made with fabric/leather uppers, but generally feature better stitching, traction and arch support. This makes them slightly heavier than Day Hikers.

Backpacker Boots are made for distance hiking. Unlike their lighter cousins, they usually have all leather uppers for more durability and support. They also require a short breaking-in period to mold to your individual foot shape. For this reason, you should purchase your boots well in advance of your hike and wear them for a few days with the socks you intend to use on the trail.

Foot Care

You cannot enjoy your hike if your feet are miserable. There are several things you can do to ensure your comfort:

1. Wear socks that ensure a proper boot fit. Many hikers prefer to wear a light polypropylene liner sock with a heavier wool sock over it. This system absorbs shock and helps prevent blisters. The liner and outer sock will act to eliminate heel chafing, the first cause of blisters. Take enough socks to wear a clean pair every morning.

2. If you feel a hot spot on your foot, you are developing a blister. Stop and apply an adhesive bandage or moleskin to prevent a more serious problem later.

3. Pack a small wash cloth to wash your feet every night. Your feet and your tent-mate will love you for it.

4. Rub talcum powder on your feet to absorb moisture. A film vial full of talcum is lightweight and usually lasts several days.

5. Carry a nail clipper. Well-trimmed nails help discourage the discomfort of "toe jam" on steep descents.

6. Dry your boot innersoles by removing them at night. If you're on an extended trip, pack a spare pair of innersoles or have a pair waiting at a food drop to replace old ones that become compressed over time.

7. Pack a small foot care kit (containing the last 5 items) in a ditty bag so it will be easy to find at the end of the day.

Clothing

Choosing clothes for the trail is based on four criteria: warmth in relation to weight, durability, ease of care (especially on extended trips), and versatility.

Layering: The best way to ensure you're prepared for any conditions, while carrying the least amount of clothing to do the job, is to base your wardrobe on "the layering system."

Modern fabrics allow today's hiker to dress in fewer layers and with a higher degree of mobility and comfort than those of a few decades ago. The key to comfort in any conditions is a three layer system consisting of underwear, an insulating layer and a protective layer. A well-prepared hiker carries all three.

Underwear – Polyester, polypropylene or wool are most effective in transporting moisture away from the body, keeping you warm and dry. Most hikers carry lightweight polyester or polypropylene shirts and bottoms on extended trips. They weigh less and dry faster than their wool counterparts.

Insulating Layer – This layer should trap insulating air between the underwear and the protective outer layer. Synthetic fleece garments are favored by many hikers. They provide warmth, wick moisture, and air-dry quickly.

Protective Layer – This layer should shield you from rain, wind or snow, while allowing moisture to escape. Nylon or waterproof/ breathable fabrics are the most popular choices.

T-Shirts: Many hikers instinctively reach for a cotton T-Shirt when loading their backpack. While T-Shirts offer initial comfort, they often become weighed down with perspiration during the day. After a T-Shirt is wet, it may take several days to dry out. The result is added weight on the back of your pack (as you attempt to air dry it), or a heavy lump in the bottom of your pack as you wait for a sunny day or a trail-side laundromat to appear. A good solution is to carry two synthetic T-Shirts for hiking, and a cotton one to sleep in and wear around camp while your hiking shirts are airing out.

Packs

The first decision to make about packs is whether to choose an internal or external frame model.

External frame packs are often chosen for extended trips. They hold large loads comfortably and position gear away from the body for maximum ventilation.

Internal frame packs offer more freedom of body movement, making them the premier choice for skiers and off-trail enthusiasts.

The choice comes down to intended uses and personal preference. If you're anticipating a long-distance hike as a once-in-a-lifetime experience, you may want to steer toward an external frame pack. If you are going to make a lot of food drop stops and anticipate winter camping and skiing after your Appalachian Trail experience, an internal frame model is a logical choice. Many avid hikers will end up purchasing both models during their backpacking career.

Regardless of which style pack you choose:

1. Make sure it has enough room for all your gear and food. A 5000–6000 cubic inch model should be large enough to carry a week's worth.

2. Adjust the fit before you leave home. To make sure the pack is comfortable, put about 35 pounds of gear in it, then adjust all the straps, including waist, shoulder and "stabilizer" straps at hips and shoulders (if they exist). Finally, go for a short walk with your 35 lb. load. Do some bending. Climb some small hills. Make minor adjustments until the pack feels comfortable. If the pack does not feel comfortable after extensive adjustments, consider exchanging it for one that fits. If a ten minute hike causes discomfort, a string of 15 mile days will not be enjoyable.

Sleeping Bag

The two most common sleeping bag fills are goose down and synthetic fibers. The features to look for are fit, compactness when stuffed, and relative warmth.

Goose down bags are generally lighter, more compact and more expensive than synthetic bags. They also must be kept dry. A wet down bag will lose most of its thermal efficiency and may take several days to dry.

Synthetic bags maintain most of their thermal efficiency when wet. They are, in general, heavier and bulkier than comparably rated down bags.

Whichever style you choose, consider purchasing a compression sack. This "stuff sack with built-in straps" compresses the sleeping bag's size to provide more room in your pack for gear and food.

Most stuff sacks (compression or otherwise) are coated for water repellency. Even so, it's a good idea to carry a large plastic bag to wrap around your stuff sack on rainy days. It may mean the difference between a good night's sleep and a cold, disrupted one.

When you get home, store your sleeping bag in an oversize cotton sack designed for the purpose. Storing it loosely when not in use ensures that the bag will achieve "maximum loft" or insulating ability for years to come.

Ground Pad

The ground pad provides an insulating layer between your sleeping bag and the ground. Without one, your sleeping bag will lose much of its thermal efficiency.

A ground pad also cushions you from minor discomforts such as roots, rocks or the hardness of a lean-to floor.

Pads come in many varieties, from single-layer foam to self-inflating models that utilize a core of foam and trapped air to cushion you from the ground.

As with other gear, consider weight, amount of intended use, and budget when making your purchase decision.

Tent

The lean-tos along the Appalachian Trail are often full. It is wise to carry a tarp or lightweight "storm-proof" tent on all overnight trips. Some tents now come with seams water-proofed at the factory. If you own an older model, or the tent you purchased does not have factory-sealed seams, you will need to seal them yourself. Most outdoor stores sell seam sealant made for the job.

If you are purchasing a tent, look for a model with a full coverage rain fly for best storm protection. A fine-weave mesh in windows and doors helps keep your shelter free of bugs. This is especially important during black fly season in May and June.

Consider the weight and size of your tent. Some hikers prefer a model with gear space built in, others prefer the versatility of a vestibule that adds gear space when you need it.

If you intend to travel in a group, consider having one person carry the tent "body" and another carry the fly and poles. This helps distribute the load.

Stove

The use of a backpacking stove is highly recommended. It is an efficient and reliable method of preparing meals on the trail. When the weather is bad, you will be glad to have your stove with you. Wood fires are restricted to designated campsites along the Appalachian Trail.

Lightweight, reliable stoves are widely available. Among the cleanest burning stoves are those that burn "white gas." This fuel is available at most camping specialty and hardware stores in towns close to the Appalachian Trail. Some stoves will burn either white gas or unleaded fuel. These "multifuel stoves" give the hiker the option of burning the more widely available unleaded fuel, or the cleaner-burning white gas.

Butane stoves use a pressurized canister of liquefied butane. While they burn cleanly and efficiently, the potential for the butane to vaporize, the necessity to carry heavy canisters, and the uncertain availability of canisters in shops along the Trail make these stoves a second choice. Alcohol stoves, using a solid or gel-like fuel, do not provide the heating efficiency of the white gas or butane stoves.

Become familiar with your stove at home, before setting out on the Trail.

Food

No trail-related choice relies more on personal preference than your daily diet. Whether you prefer to snack all day or eat "three squares", one rule of thumb applies: ***pack the most nutrition per ounce.***

There are three basic food choices facing today's hiker:

Freeze-Dried: Increasingly varied and nutritious, freeze-dried foods are also lightweight and easy to prepare. In most cases, all you have to do is boil water, pour it into the food pouch, wait five minutes, and eat. There aren't even any pots and pans to clean up after dinner. The downside to these fast, easy meals is that they are expensive. However, a few freeze-dried meals can serve as a quick meal after a high-mileage day or an extra meal in case you're on the trail a day longer than you had planned.

Air Dried: Health food and grocery stores often carry dried fruits and vegetables that make nutritious trail snacks or additions to one pot meals. You may also want to consider drying your own food at home. You can buy a food dehydrator, build one, or dry food in your conventional oven with the door ajar to let moisture escape. Your local library will be able to provide more information about food drying at home.

Supermarket: You can create an endless variety of light-weight, nutritious trail meals by browsing the aisles of your local supermarket.

Small (fast cooking) sizes of pasta and quick cooking rice are popular trail staples to build one pot meals around. Sauces and gravy mixes are easily packed and add a lot of flavor. Don't forget the spices. Film vials filled with pepper, oregano and other spices can give a previously bland meal some gourmet flare.

When creating your trail menu, keep in mind that foods high in carbohydrates and fats provide sustained energy, while sugar-based foods generate a short term energy boost. It is a good idea to balance your diet accordingly.

A few more food considerations:

- One pot meals are easier to prepare and use less fuel than more complicated meals.
- A short wooden spoon is light and indispensable for preparing such meals.
- Plan lunches that do not require cooking. Routinely "breaking out the stove" adds at least an extra hour to your lunch break and requires you to carry 1/3 more fuel.

Packaging: Before you hit the trail, take the time to repackage your foods, eliminating excess weight and waste. Zip-seal plastic bags come in handy for this. Some hikers pack breakfast, lunch and dinner supplies into separate stuff sacks to make them easy to find at meal time and easy to hang out of the reach of animals at night.

A large zip-seal bag serves well as a personal "litter bag" during your hike and for picking up what less thoughtful visitors may have left behind.

Helpful Hints

Carry your clothing and food in different colored stuff sacks to help you keep gear organized and make finding it easier.

Always carry plenty of water. Two quarts per person per day is a good rule of thumb. Take drinks often to stay fully hydrated.

Fill your canteens before you hit the trail. It is better to drink tap water than to rely solely on backcountry sources.

Practice minimum impact camping. Carry out whatever you pack in so others can enjoy the surroundings.

Suggested Reading

The following books may be useful for planning your hike or determining equipment needs:

The Complete Walker III, by Colin Fletcher, Alfred A. Knopf, New York, NY, 1984.

The Appalachian Trail Thru-Hikers' Companion, edited by Bill O'Brien, Appalachian Trail Conference, Harpers Ferry, WV, (updated annually).

The Thru-Hiker's Planning Guide, by Dan "Wingfoot" Bruce, Center for Appalachian Trail Studies, High Point, N.C. 1994.

The Appalachian Trail Backpacker, by Victoria and Frank Logue, Menasha Ridge Press, Birmingham, AL, 1994.

For a more extensive list of hiking books write to:
The Appalachian Trail Conference
P.O. Box 807
Harpers Ferry, WV 25425-0807

CAMPFIRES

The Appalachian Trail passes through the vast "working forest" of Maine. Almost all of the land along the Trail corridor is managed for the commercial production of timber. It is of critical importance, both to preserve the physical environment of the Trail and to protect the forests along the Trail, that every reasonable precaution be taken to avoid forest fires.

All A.T. campsites shown on the accompanying maps are approved public campsites designated by the Maine Bureau of Forestry. No permit is required to build a fire in the fireplace provided at each site. Wood fires may not be built at any other locations along the Appalachian Trail in Maine. On occasion, the Governor issues a proclamation closing the woods to all smoking and open air burning. When that occurs, wood fires in fireplaces at designated campsites and lean-tos are absolutely prohibited.

No permits are required for backpackers' stoves along the A.T. in Maine. *The MATC strongly encourages the use of portable stoves.*

If you must build a fire:
• Use the fireplace provided.
• Use only dead, fallen wood; do not cut live trees.
• Keep the fire small — only as large as needed.
• NEVER leave a fire unattended.
• Drown your campfire before leaving.
• Leave only ashes in the fireplace.
• Carry out any unburned trash. (Aluminum foil will not burn).

This message regarding fires is important enough to repeat: *Anyone who leaves a fire unattended which gets out of control and causes damage is legally responsible for all the costs of both fire suppression and property damage (including timber value). Be sure your fire is "dead out" when you leave it.*

LEAN-TOS AND CAMPSITES

There is a complete chain of campsites along the Appalachian Trail from Katahdin to the Maine–New Hampshire border. Most of these sites have a lean-to, an outhouse, and a fireplace. Those sites which do not have a lean-to include a fireplace, an outhouse, and, in some cases, tent platforms. Each site is identified by signs.

The shelters in Maine are Adirondack style lean-tos, an open front, roofed structure constructed of logs. A raised sleeping platform, or "bunk", also serves as the lean-to floor. Space to sit is provided here or on the front log known as the "deacon seat." Older lean-tos or those damaged by accidents of nature or malicious mischief may leak. Please keep your self and your gear off the lean-to roof. The shelters in Maine are built and maintained by volunteers. If you find a lean-to in need of repair, please let us know.

The lean-to facilities are provided for the backpacker who may have no other means of shelter. Anyone planning an overnight hike is encouraged to carry and use a tent. This is good insurance, since the Trail is heavily used, and the shelters are usually crowded during the summer months. Camps and other organizations such as Scouts, wilderness experience programs, or educational institutions are asked to limit their groups to less than ten including leaders. Groups should carry tents and not monopolize the lean-to or fireplace.

Although shelter use is on a "first come, first served" basis, Trail etiquette dictates that there is always room for one more, particularly in inclement weather.

Lean-tos are provided for overnight stays only, and, except for reasons of weather, injury, or other emergency, hikers are asked not to stay more than two nights. Hunters, fishermen and other non-Trail hikers are asked not to use the lean-tos for a base of operations.

Lean-tos and campsites concentrate Trail users and thus require considerate use by all. Noise should be kept to a minimum from dusk to dawn. Use the facilities with care and respect and refrain from using an axe or a jackknife on any part of the lean-to. Do not use the "deacon seat" as a chopping block.

MATC lean-to maintainers provide a register to gather

information and comments from hikers. Often there will be another notebook in the lean-to placed there by hikers for other hikers to leave messages. Registers placed in lean-tos by the MATC belong to the MATC. Hikers should not expect the registers to be forwarded to them when they are full.

Information about individual lean-tos and campsites and the distances between them are found on the Trail description side of each map.

Toilet facilities at most campsites are open pit privies with a spring-closing door and screened ventilation under the eaves. Outhouses are located the shortest distance from the campsite that soil conditions will allow. At Horns Pond on Bigelow Mountain, a large batch-bin composting system is being used since soil conditions and altitude make it difficult for a normal privy to function properly. It is essential that hikers use the outhouses to ensure the sanitary condition of each campsite. Always be sure an outhouse door is closed when you leave. Porcupines are fond of chewing on the wood of an outhouse and significant structural damage is often the result!

The source of water for a campsite may be a lake, a stream, or a spring. No source of water can be trusted to be safe for consumption without treatment. Every precaution should be taken to avoid contaminating the water supply and the surrounding area.

Lean-tos and designated campsites have been authorized by the Maine Forestry Department and do not require a permit to build a fire in the fireplace provided. Wood fires are NOT permitted anywhere else along the Trail.

The use of backpacking stoves is highly encouraged. In foul weather they are by far the easiest means of boiling water or cooking a meal. Camping facilities along the trail have been located with particular attention to preserving the ecology of the area. It is important that any firewood collected be "dead and down." This will necessitate going some distance for firewood. Cutting of standing timber is not permitted. Common sense dictates that campfires be kept to a minimum. When you leave the campsite be sure your fire is "dead out."

Careful trip and meal planning will make it easier to leave your campsite without a trace. The Carry In – Carry Out rule applies to all refuse. Before the advent of Reduce–Reuse–Recycle, when every town in Maine had an open garbage dump, a popular pastime was to go down to the dump after dark to watch the black bears. Those days should be history. Plan ahead, keep your refuse to a minimum and if you carry it in, carry it out.

SUGGESTED HIKES

The following tables list suggested trips along the A.T. in Maine by map. You will find additional information on the maps and in Chapter 6 of this Guide. Enterprising trip planners will devise numerous combinations or extensions of these trips and are encouraged to do so.

The hikes outlined below are arranged starting with Map 1 (including Katahdin at the north end of the Appalachian Trail) and continuing southward to Map 7 (ending on the Maine–New Hampshire border). Day trips are listed first, followed by the overnight trips for each section. Distances given are round trip mileage for day trips requiring a return by the same route. Mileage for trips longer than one day and for circuit or loop trips is one way only.

TRIP	DISTANCE (ROUND TRIP)	FEATURES	STARTS/ENDS
MAP 1	*Section 1*		
Baxter Peak	10.4 mi.	Highest peak in Me. Terminus of A.T. (start early)	Katahdin Stream Campground
Katahdin Stream Falls	2.4 mi.	Mountain stream and waterfalls	Katahdin Stream Campground
The Owl	6.6 mi.	Outstanding views of Witherle Ravine on Katahdin	Katahdin Stream Campground
Sentinel Mtn.	6.4 mi.	Panoramic views of Katahdin and Mtns. to N	Daicey Pond Campground Road
Big and Little Niagara Falls	2.4 mi.	Toll Dam and two outstanding waterfalls	Daicey Pond Campground
	Section 2		
Pollywog Gorge (circuit with road walk)	3.9 mi. (may vary with condition of access rd.)	Scenic gorge, site of historic log drives	Gravel road at South-bound mileage point 17.4 or 20.0
Nesuntabunt Mountain	2.4 mi. (may vary with condition of access rd.)	Remote area with views of many lakes to the east and Katahdin to the north	Gravel road at Southbound mileage point 20.0
Abol Bridge to Katahdin	15.1 mi. (one way) *2 days*	Nesowadnehunk Stream, Daicey Pond and Katahdin	Abol Bridge area
Abol Bridge to Jo-Mary Road	40.8 mi. (one way) *3–5 days*	The lakes trip — visits several of the largest lakes along the A.T.	A.T. from Abol Bridge (Map 1) or Jo-Mary Road (Map 2)

TRIP	DISTANCE (ROUND TRIP)	FEATURES	STARTS/ENDS
MAP 2	*Section 3*		
White Cap Mountain	6.0 mi. (may vary with condition of access rd.)	Excellent views N to Katahdin and SW to the mtns. of western Maine	A.T. from West Branch Ponds Road
White Cap Mountain	5.8 mi. (may vary with condition of access rd.)	Excellent views N to Katahdin and SW to the mtns. of western Maine	White Brook Trail and A.T. from Katahdin Iron Works
Gulf Hagas	8.2 mi.	The Hermitage, the spectacular Gulf (gorge) and its many waterfalls	Trail parking on main haul road 6.7 mi. W of Katahdin Iron Works
Gulf Hagas and the White Cap Range	varies depending on route. *2–3 days*	Spectacular gorge and waterfalls and excellent views N to Katahdin and SW to the mtns. of western Maine	A.T. at Gulf Hagas to fork of West Branch Ponds Road
MAP 3	*Section 4*		
Chairback Mountain	7.8 mi.	Views of White Cap Range to the north	Trail parking on main haul road 6.7 mi. W of Katahdin Iron Works
Barren Mountain	11.2 mi. (varies w/ condition of access rd.)	Outstanding views from White Cap to the mountains of western Maine, Slugundy Falls	Bodfish Farm Site off Elliotsville Road, Monson

TRIP	DISTANCE (ROUND TRIP)	FEATURES	STARTS/ENDS
MAP 3	*Section 4*		
Barren – Chairback Range	17.8 mi. (one way) *2–3 days*	Delightful range walk, several mountain tarns, good views from the five peaks	Trail parking 6.7 mi. w of Katahdin Iron Works to Bodfish Farm Site
100 Mile "Wilderness"	99.4 mi. (one way) *8–10 days*	Scenic, wild country, the remote part of the entire A.T.	Abol Bridge (Map 1) to Me. Highway 15, Monson (Map 3)
MAP 4	*Section 5*		
Moxie Bald Mountain	9.8 mi. (add 2.8 mi. round trip to North Peak)	Excellent views and good blueberries from mid to end of summer	A.T. from Moxie Pond
Pleasant Pond Mountain	3.2 mi.	Good views from summit ledges, swimming in Pleasant Pond	A. T. from logging road near Pleasant Pond
Horseshoe Canyon to Moxie Bald Mountain	18.5 mi. (one way) *2–3 days*	Horseshoe Canyon, old-growth forest, and excellent views from summit of Moxie Bald	Shirley – Blanchard Rd. Monson to Moxie Pond Road

TRIP	DISTANCE (ROUND TRIP)	FEATURES	STARTS/ENDS
MAP 5	*Section 6*		
Pierce Pond Stream	up to 6.0 mi.	Stream and many waterfalls	Gravel road 19.4 mi. N of Bingham
	Section 7		
Carry Ponds	17.2 mi. (one way) *2 days*	Scenic ponds, waterfalls and historic Arnold Trail route	Kennebec River to Long Falls Dam Rd.
Little Bigelow Mountain	4.8 mi. (Eastern peak)	1.4 mile long semi-open summit ridge	A.T. from East Flagstaff Rd.
Avery Peak, Bigelow Mountain	8.0 mi.	Exc. views from Canadian Border Mtns. to White Mtns. of NH	Safford Brook Trail from East Flafstaff Road
Bigelow Mountain (circuit)	12.4 mi. (add 0.8 mi. to incl. Avery Pk.)	Outstanding views from the crest of West Pk. and South Horn on Bigelow	Fire Warden's and Horns Pond Trails, Stratton Brook Pond Road
Bigelow Mountain (circuit)	12.5 mi. (incl. 0.7 mi. road walk)	Outstanding views from the crest of West Pk. and South Horn on Bigelow	A.T. and Fire Warden's Trail, Stratton Brook Pond Road
Cranberry Peak	5.8 mi.	Good views of surrounding mtns. of western Me.	Bigelow Range Trail, Stratton

TRIP	DISTANCE (ROUND TRIP)	FEATURES	STARTS/ENDS
MAP 6	*Section 8*		
Crocker Mountain	12.4 mi.	Good views of mtns. of western Me.	A.T. from Me. Highway 27
Sugarloaf Mountain	5.8 mi. (varies w/ condition of access rd)	Second highest peak in Maine Outstanding views and glacial cirque	A.T. and side trail, from Caribou Valley Road
Saddleback Mountain	11.4 mi.	Outstanding views of mtns. of western Me. and Rangeley Lakes area	A.T. from Me. Highway 4
4,000 footer trip	36.8 mi. (one way) *3–5 days*	The Crockers, Sugarloaf, Mt. Abraham, and the Saddleback Range	A.T. from Me. Highway 27 to Me. Highway 4 incl. side trails
	Section 9		
Traverse of Section 9	13.1 mi. (one way) *1–2 days*	Five highland ponds, several boreal bogs, and sand beach	A.T. from Me. Highway 4 to Me. Highway 17
MAP 7	*Section 10*		
Bemis Mountain (circuit)	13.9 mi. (incl. 0.5 mi. road walk) *1–2 days*	Partially open ridge, and pleasant streamside walk	A.T. from Me. Highway 17 return via Bemis Stream Trail
Old Blue Mountain	5.6 mi.	Excellent views of mtns. of western Me.	A.T. from South Arm Rd.

TRIP	DISTANCE (ROUND TRIP)	FEATURES	STARTS/ENDS
MAP 7	*Section 12*		
Dunn Notch (circuit)	2.1 mi. (incl. side trails to falls)	Dunn Notch and spectacular waterfalls	Via Cascade Trail and A.T. from East B Hill Road
Baldpate – East and West Peaks	8.0 mi.	Outstanding views in all directions from East Peak	A.T. from Me. Highway 26 in Grafton Notch
Table Rock (circuit)	2.4 mi.	Good views of Grafton Notch from top of cliff, in Grafton Notch slab caves	A.T. and Table Rock Tr. from Me. Highway 26 in Grafton Notch
	Section 13		
The Eyebrow	2.3 mi.	Views of Grafton Notch, Table Rock, and Baldpate Mtn.	A.T. and Eyebrow Trail from Me. Highway 26 in Grafton Notch
Old Speck	7.6 mi.	Third highest peak in Maine. Excellent views from tower platform	A.T. and side trail from Me. Highway 26 in Grafton Notch
Mahoosuc Range — Old Speck to Goose Eye	16.2 mi. (one way) *2 days*	Third highest peak in Maine, Mahoosuc Notch, and high boreal bogs	A.T. and side trail from Me. Highway 26 in Grafton Notch
Mahoosuc Range	31.3 mi. (one way) *3–5 days*	Outstanding ridge traverse	A.T. and side trail from Me. Highway 26 in Grafton Notch to U.S. Rt. 2, Shelburne, N.H.

TRANSPORTATION TO THE TRAIL

Highway Access

Most of the Trail in Maine is readily accessible by vehicle with the notable exception of the northern stretch between Monson and Abol Bridge. A general access map for the area south of the Kennebec River is provided on Map 6; a similar map for most of the area north of the Kennebec is on Map 4. For any road access, the *Maine Atlas and Gazetteer* available from DeLorme Publishing, P.O. Box 298, Freeport, ME 04032, is an invaluable aid.

The southernmost 180 miles of Trail in Maine crosses nine public all-weather roads. Most highway maps show these roads. These accesses provide flexibility for planning trips of varying length.

The northernmost hundred miles of the Trail crosses several private logging roads and one public road. These are seasonal roads, generally accessible from May to November. The quality of these roads varies considerably from hard-surfaced gravel to barely passable with four-wheel drive. Some of the roads are open to the public, others may be used for a fee, and some require advanced arrangements to pass through a control gate. Specific information and directions for access are provided on each map accompanying this book. Many of the roads are not shown on a state highway map. Trail access on the back roads of Maine can change rapidly depending on weather and logging activity.

Bus Lines

Bus routes offer no access to the Trail itself. There are several connecting links which can be valuable. The major bus lines, Greyhound and Trailways offer service to Portland and Bangor. From Bangor, the local Cyr Bus Line goes to Medway, 10 miles east of Millinocket; Cyr's phone: (207) 827-2335. A van service may be available from the Bangor bus station to Dover-Foxcroft.

Railroads

At press time there are plans to extend passenger rail service from Boston to Portland. Contact your travel agent for current information.

Air Service

Major airlines serve the international airports at Portland and Bangor. Daily shuttle service is also available to Lewiston, Augusta, and Waterville.

Several large lakes make float plane service a viable method of transportation to the Trail, particularly in northern Maine, and to a lesser extent in central and western Maine. Float planes typically carry from 1 to 3 passengers with gear. Operators serving the A.T. include:

Katahdin Air Service, Millinocket; Phone: (207) 723-8378
Central Maine Flying Service, Old Town; Phone: (207) 827-5911
Folsom's Air Service, Greenville; Phone: (207) 695-2821
Twitchell's Airport, Turner; Phone: (207) 225-3490

Taxi and Shuttle Service

In most towns within fifty miles of the Trail, it is possible to arrange transportation to a trailhead with a local taxi company or service station.

Shaw's Boarding Home, in Monson, offers a hiker's shuttle service. Inquire locally for shuttle services which may be available in other areas.

Other Sources of Information

A Chamber of Commerce is available in each of the following towns/areas: Bethel, Bingham, Farmington, Greenville, Guilford, Millinocket, Milo, Rangeley, Rumford, Skowhegan, and the Sugarloaf area in Kingfield.

FIRST AID ON THE TRAIL
by Ned Claxton, M.D.

Along the Appalachian Trail in Maine, a hiker will meet a wide variety of terrain and climatic conditions. In planning the safe trip, it is only common sense to "Be Prepared" for the unexpected.

Preparation

Many situations which have the potential to become serious first aid problems can be prevented. Every hiking group should carry a first aid kit and should include someone who has recently taken courses in First Aid and Cardiopulmonary Resuscitation (CPR). Courses are offered in most communities by the American National Red Cross. Specialized courses focusing on wilderness medical skills are also available in many areas. These courses require your active participation in learning proper first aid response. Some techniques such as artificial respiration (rescue breathing) and CPR are beyond the scope of this guidebook.

The information in this section of the Guide is in no way a substitute for proper first aid training. It can only serve as a reminder or a ready reference if a medical emergency occurs.

Analysis of serious accidents has shown that a substantial number of them have their origin "back home" in the planning stage of the trip.

Before your trip, think about communications. Have you informed relatives or friends about your expedition — when you will leave, what your itinerary is, and your expected time of return? Have you carefully checked the condition of all of your equipment? Consider both the season and the potential weather at the higher elevations when planning your trip. Have you made provisions for water, food, warmth, and shelter? Remember, emergency situations can develop quickly. When you get out on the trail, set a comfortable pace for the group and see that the entire party practices good trail discipline.

If a hiker is lost, a storm strikes, or an accident occurs, S.T.O.P.

Stop
Think
Observe
Plan

Remember, the brain is your most important survival tool.

First Aid Kit

The following first aid kit is suggested for those who have had minimal first aid or other medical training. It costs under $70, weighs about a pound and occupies about a 3" X 6" X 9" space.

2	pair of latex gloves
12	4" X 4" non-adherent gauze pad dressings
5	2" elastic Band-Aid® strips
10	1" elastic Band-Aid® strips
6	alcohol prep pads
1	tube of Aloe Vera (relief for burns)
3	large Steri-Strips® (replace butterfly closures)
1	triangular bandage (40")
2	3" rolls of gauze
20	acetaminophen, aspirin, or ibuprofen tablets
1	roll waterproof adhesive tape, 2" X 15'
1	4" elastic bandage (or self adhering type)
2	3" X 4" moleskin® pads and Second Skin®
3	safety pins
1	pair of rugged bandage scissors
1	pair of tweezers for splinters
1	tube antiseptic first aid cream
1	needle
1	SAM® splint (light weight, roll up)
1	oral thermometer
	personal medications as necessary depending on length of trip and availability of emergency care

In the Field

The following section, arranged alphabetically for easy reference, suggests methods of prevention and provides recommendations for first aid treatment.

In any medical emergency, before you proceed to help the injured, be sure that the scene is free of hazards that may injure you. As you survey the scene, look for the method of injury. Was it a fall, was it a rock slide, or was it the result of hot or cold temperatures?

Patient Assessment

When assessing a patient's condition you first need to check and see if the patient has an open airway, is breathing, and has a pulse. Techniques such as artificial respiration (rescue breathing) and CPR are beyond the scope of this guide. If you lack these skills, seek the help of others, nearby or in another group, who are properly trained.

Examine the person carefully, noting all possible injuries. It is important to do a head to toe survey so that you do not focus your energy on only the most readily observable injury and miss one that may be more critical.

The injured will need encouragement, assurance of help and promotion of confidence by the demonstration of your competency. Treat the injured gently. Keep the victim lying down and quiet. Protect the person from the weather with insulation both below and above. *Always treat for shock* — not doing so can turn relatively minor injuries into life threatening situations.

If outside help is needed at least one person should stay with the injured hiker; two people, if possible, should go for help and carry with them written notes including an assessment of the patient's condition. An *Accident Report Form* is located at the back of this book for completion in the event of an accident.

Back Or Neck Injuries

Signs and symptoms of spinal injuries can include pain in the spine or a spine that is tender to the touch. *Do not move the victim unless it is absolutely necessary.* The spinal cord can be severed with inexpert handling. This type of injury must be handled by a large group of experienced personnel. *Outside help must be obtained.*

Immobilize the entire body where the victim lies, move him/her, as directed below, to a level, firm surface and get assistance. If you need to roll the person over, roll the body as a unit keeping the head in line with the spine and legs. Protect the head and neck from movement if a neck injury is suspected. Treat for shock and as a fracture. Transportation should be on a rigid frame, such as a litter.

Bleeding

Create a barrier between yourself and the victim's blood fluids by wearing latex gloves. Stop the bleeding with direct pressure over the wound. Use several sterile compresses (4" X 4" sterile gauze pads), if available, directly over the wound. If bleeding persists, cover with sterile gauze and wrap tightly with a continuous bandage. Do not obstruct circulation to the rest of the limb. Loosen the bandage if bluish discoloration of the nail beds (normally pink tissue under nails), excessive pain, numbness, or swelling are noted beyond the bandage. Splinting can also be used to immobilize a wound on a joint.

Apply a tourniquet only in cases of amputation (loss of hand, leg or foot). If there is a traumatic amputation, place the tourniquet between the injury and the heart just above the site of amputation. WARNING, once applied, the tourniquet should only be removed by medical personnel equipped to stop the bleeding by other means and to restore lost blood.

Blisters

Take good care of your feet, they are vital to your well-being. Good boot fit, without points of irritation or pressure, should be proven before a hike. Be aware of the comfort of your feet as you are hiking. Liner socks made of polypropylene help to move perspiration away from the foot and into the outer boot sock allowing the boot sock to slide over the foot more easily, and helping to prevent blisters. Respond to developing hot spots by placing adhesive tape or moleskin over the area. Relieve irritation if possible, and allow blister fluid to be absorbed. If a blister pocket forms and it is necessary to open it, wash the area with soap and water and prick the edge of the blister with a needle that has been sterilized in the flame of a match. Apply an antiseptic cream and a sterile gauze pad or moleskin and change the bandage at least daily.

Bone Fractures Of Arms, Legs, Or Ankles

Fractures may be obvious by inspection, but even if you only suspect a fracture, it must be splinted before moving the victim. After treating for shock and dressing wounds, use any available material that will offer firm support such as tree branches or boards. Pad each side of the arm or leg including the joints above and below the injury, and immobilize the injured limb with soft material. A SAM® splint is ideal or use strips of cloth or clothing rolled to 1 inch in diameter to bind the splints together. Attempt to keep fractures elevated as much as possible and apply ice or cold cloths to minimize swelling. Be sure to check circulation below the splinted area regularly, as swelling associated with the injury can cause the splint to impede circulation.

Burns

Take care around any fire, particularly with hot liquids. If an accident should occur, the first aid for any burn involves a few basic principles: Cool the area with cool water for up to 15–20 minutes to prevent deeper damage from occurring.

For surface area burns that are red (first degree) or blistered (second degree), clean with soap and water, apply an antibiotic ointment and cover loosely with dry sterile dressings to prevent infection. Treat for shock.

More serious burns (third degree), include those that are brown or black in color, those that cover more than one area of the body, or those where the victim has difficulty breathing. Third degree burns may be potentially life threatening and require the attention of medical personnel. First aid for more serious burns is: clean with soap and water, cover loosely with dry sterile dressings, treat for shock, and seek medical help.

Choking

If food or a foreign body is lodged in the air passage, and coughing does not dislodge it, try to remove the object with your fingers. If the blockage is not accessible and the patient can't talk, the Heimlich maneuver may be used to dislodge the object. Stand behind the person with your arms around their waist, well below the breast bone, and give a quick, abrupt squeeze up into the chest. If the person has collapsed, you may need to kneel to push up into the chest with the palm of your hand.

Cold Temperature Hazards

Temperatures can drop quickly in Maine, particularly at higher elevations in the spring and fall. Even in the summer, wind chill can be lethal in highly exposed places. Alcohol and tobacco should be avoided as they can make thermal injuries even more severe. A number of deaths have occurred above treeline on New England mountains from loss of body heat by wind and wetness. The wind-chill chart at end of Chapter 1 provides a clear view of the relationship between wind and temperature loss.

Hypothermia is a decrease in the body core temperature causing impairment of normal muscular and brain functioning. Early stages of hypothermia can include marked fatigue, shivering, irritability, or a generally cold feeling. Lack of muscular coordination begins when body temperature drops to 98° F and becomes obvious below 95° F along with mental confusion. Loss of consciousness and death can occur below 82° F. Important contributing factors are bad weather, insufficient or wet clothing, lack of food, and fatigue. Always carry spare dry clothing, extra food and a waterproof shell layer. Wool or synthetic fleece and polypropylene are the best choices because they lose little of their insulating properties when wet. Never start across a long stretch above treeline unless you are well fed and rested.

For mild stages of hypothermia, STOP and get the victim into dry, warm clothing including a hat and gloves. Offer quick energy foods high in sugars, and warm fluids if the victim is conscious. Have the person exercise to increase heat production. If this is not possible, have someone get into a sleeping bag with the victim. Close bodily contact will provide rapid warmth.

In the case of severe hypothermia the person's level of consciousness will be significantly reduced to the point of being unresponsive. You must act quickly to prevent further heat loss. Wrap the person in pre-warmed dry insulation and mild heat packs. Do not give food or fluids to an unconscious person.

Frostnip is a mild, reversible cold injury. Prevention includes adequate warm clothing, proper hydration and feeding, and wind protection. The chilled part should be covered and can be warmed by direct contact with warm, bare flesh. A cheek, nose, or chin can often be protected from the wind by covering with your hand. Hands can be warmed by placing in the armpits, on the stomach, or in the groin area.

Frostbite is an actual freezing of the affected body tissues, most often the hands, feet, nose, ears, or face. The earliest sign of frostbite is a pale color to the skin tissue which becomes white, or ashen gray as frostbite advances.

Do not rub frozen flesh. Cover it with layers of wool or any other good insulating material. The best treatment is rapid re-warming in a hot water bath of 105–108° F. This is not practical in the field due to the difficulty in maintaining a large pot of water at the precise temperature, the extreme pain caused by thawing, and the risk of infection. If frozen flesh is to be thawed, it must not be allowed to re-freeze. Never warm a frozen foot or hand over an open fire as this cooks the flesh.

A victim of frostbite should seek medical attention as soon as possible.

If emergency shelter is needed in cold weather, get out of the wind and under logs or blowdowns, or into a cave, snow pit shelter, or pit shelter dug next to a tree. Get a wood fire going, if possible, and change into dry clothing.

Dislocation Of A Leg Or Arm Joint

Dislocations are usually extremely painful. Do not try to put it back in place. Immobilize the entire limb by splinting it in the position it is found. You may need to use great ingenuity in devising supports, bandaging, and transporting the patient for medical attention. Remember to treat for shock.

Giardia

Giardia lamblia is a microscopic water-borne parasite that causes a prolonged infection known as Giardiasis. Ingestion of the cyst and its growth in the intestines of mammals is part of the life cycle of Giardia. Treating all of your drinking water is the best way to avoid the "beaver fever." While the disease is not normally life threatening to humans, its symptoms can be very uncomfortable and sometimes incapacitating. The incubation period, between ingestion and symptoms, can last from a week to a couple of months. The fatigue and weight loss resulting from the infection can last from one to three weeks. If you experience fatigue, weight loss, and persistent diarrhea, notify your doctor that you may have Giardiasis.

Heat Emergencies

Exposure to extreme high temperatures, high humidity and direct sunlight may cause various types of health problems associated with the temperature of the body.

Heat Exhaustion is a form of shock. Physical exercise and a prolonged exposure to hot, or humid weather can cause a rapid loss of fluids in the body though sweating. This can affect even those in excellent physical condition. Rapid fluid loss causes an insufficient supply of blood to reach vital areas such as the brain, heart and lungs. The skin can be moist and cool, a flushed face turns pale; the victim may feel faint, complain of a headache and dizziness, or feel a pounding heart. As heat exhaustion progresses the patient may vomit, become delirious, or lose consciousness. Treat the victim by moving him/her to a shaded place. Administer cold fluids if the victim is conscious. Loosen or remove clothing, and apply cool wet cloths or fan the moist skin to provide rapid cooling. If not cared for promptly, heat exhaustion can progress to the more dangerous heat stroke.

Heat Stroke is caused by the failure of the heat regulatory system to sufficiently cool the body. This is an emergency situation and is life-threatening. The body temperature may go to 105° F or higher. The onset of initial symptoms is very rapid and includes weakness, nausea, and heat cramps. The temperature rises rapidly and sweat glands cease to function. The skin is dry and hot; the pulse is rapid, but may be difficult to detect. The victim becomes delirious or unconscious. Treatment must be immediate or fatal brain damage will occur. Immerse the victim in tepid, not cold, water, or remove clothing and cover with cool cloths, fanning to promote evaporation. Meanwhile, massage the extremities and beware of causing hypothermia. Vigorous cooling efforts should cease when body temperature reaches 102° F. Monitor the victim carefully to prevent a recurrence.

Insect Bites

Insects can be a hazard in the woods. Ground nesting "yellow jackets" have surprised a few hikers, and can produce painful stings. If you are severely allergic to bee stings you should carry the necessary anaphylaxis kit, available by prescription. If you are mildly allergic you may want to carry an "after-bite" treatment available from your pharmacy. If you are stung by bees, take care to travel out of their immediate range, and then remove the stinger with tweezers or a knife.

Wood ticks, which are about the size of lentils, can be a problem in grassy areas. They are slow to attach themselves and are easily picked off from clothing or skin. Once they are attached, it is most effective to touch the tick with a hot match causing it to back out, or grip the tick with tweezers near the surface of your skin. Wash the bite, use an antiseptic cream, and cover it to prevent infection.

Mosquitoes, black flies, and no-see-ums tend to be far more pesky. A good insect repellent is a necessity in May and June, and recommended in July and August. Rubbing alcohol or a hydrocortisone cream may relieve the itching.

Lyme Disease

Lyme disease is rare in the mountains of Maine, but is more common in southern New England and spreading northward. It is transmitted by the bite of a deer tick, about the size of the head of a pin. The tick must stay attached for about 6 hours to transmit the disease. Symptoms of the disease include: headache, fever, vomiting, muscle soreness and fatigued joints. The rash developing around the bite may form concentric rings or even irregular shaped patterns on other parts of the body. If you experience these symptoms even days or weeks after a trip, let your doctor know you may have Lyme disease. However, one quarter of all people with an infected tick bite show none of the early symptoms. When caught early, the disease can be successfully treated with antibiotics. If left untreated, the effects of the disease can be very severe including severe fatigue, dizziness, shortness of breath, cardiac irregularities, memory and concentration problems, facial paralysis, meningitis, shooting pains in the arms and legs, and other even more severe mental problems.

Poison Ivy

The poison ivy plant is quite adaptable and most prolific along the Trail. It can grow as a low plant, a small shrub, or a woody vine in open sunny areas or in moist shady areas. Avoidance is the best policy, and "leaflets three, let it be" is a good rule, but any hiker on the A.T. should be able to identify poison ivy. The poison is a non-volatile oily substance. All parts of the plant contain the poison even after long drying, but growth in which the sap is abundant is the greatest source of infection. Poisoning is caused by touching or brushing against the plant. The oil is very persistent, and can be carried on your clothing, equipment or pets. Contact with the oils usually causes an allergic reaction that begins with a rash and may lead to weeping blisters. Wash the exposed areas of the skin using a non-moisturizing soap. Apply a poison ivy lotion available at any pharmacy. If this solution does not control the rash within a few days, or the face is involved, seek medical help before it becomes more serious.

Shock

Shock can occur as a result of *any* injury, dehydration, or severe infection. Signs of shock are paleness, trembling, cool skin, increased respiration, and rapid pulse. If the person can be safely moved, have him/her lie flat on the back, position the head slightly downhill or raise the feet slightly. Keep the person as warm and comfortable as possible. Protect from the wind.

Sprains

An over-stretching of muscles or supporting structures around the joint is a sprain. The joint most commonly injured by hikers is the ankle, which becomes swollen and tender. Treat with ice or cold cloths, rest, elevation, and an elastic wrap. A severe sprain will have to be splinted like a fracture.

Sunburn

The best prevention for sunburn is a good sunscreen, a hat, and limited exposure to the sun. Sunscreens with an SPF (sun protection factor) of 15 to 25 are generally adequate on exposed skin for all but the fairest of complexions. Total sun blocks such as titanium dioxide or zinc oxide will prevent both burning and tanning on sensitive areas like the nose, lips and ears. Treat sunburn with cold, wet dressings soaked in a boric acid solution (1 tsp. to 1 quart of water). Aloe vera also helps to relieve the burning sensation. Keep the area covered with loose clothing.

Wounds

Abrasions, lacerations, or punctures should be cleaned with soap and water or disinfectant. If there is significant bleeding, direct pressure over the wound may stem the flow. Always have a barrier (preferably latex gloves) between yourself and a victim's blood when giving first aid. Apply a clean dressing to protect the wound from further contamination. To prevent infected wounds from becoming more serious you should have a tetanus shot every 5 to 10 years.

Suggested Reading

American Red Cross First Aid Manuals, American National Red Cross.

Medicine For Mountaineering edited by James A. Wilkerson, M.D., published by The Mountaineers, Seattle, WA.

The Outward Bound Wilderness First Aid Book by Jeff Isaac & Peter Goth, M.D., Lyons and Burford, New York, 1991.

WIND CHILL CHART

This chart illustrates the important relationship between wind and temperature and their combined effect on the human body.

Wind Chill Equivalent Temperature

Temp in °F	← Wind velocity →			
	15mph	25mph	35mph	45mph
60	50	45	40	35
50	40	35	30	25
40	30	25	20	15
30	20	15	10	5
20	10	0	-5	-10
10	0	-15	-25	-30
0	-15	-30	-40	-45
-10	-30	-45	-65	-70
-20	-40	-60	-75	-85
-30	-55	-85	-85	-95

FIELD GUIDE TO WIND VELOCITY

The following information may assist you in determining the wind speed without the use of a hand held anemometer.

Observed conditions / Wind Velocity (mph)

Observed conditions	Wind Velocity (mph)
If smoke rises nearly vertically	< 2
If smoke shows wind direction	5
Small twigs move constantly	10
Branches move	15
Small trees move, tents flap in breeze	20
Large branches move, tents are taut	25–30
Whole trees move	30–35
Twigs break from trees, walking is difficult	40–45
Branches are ripped from trees	45–50
Trees are uprooted	60–75
Hurricane warnings are posted	75

2
Plants and Animals of the Appalachian Trail Corridor in Maine

by David B. Field

This brief account is intended to offer the hiker some idea of the rich diversity of natural life along the Appalachian Trail in Maine. It provides no detailed descriptions, but those with some experience, plus a reasonable degree of intuition, will be able to identify many specimens. Many plants and animals have several common names. Scientific names are included for those who wish to identify species accurately.

The narrative of the plants and animals found along the Trail begins at the Maine–New Hampshire border and continues north to Katahdin. Except for certain old-growth trees and alpine communities, the species described will be found throughout the A.T. corridor in Maine. The list is by no means exhaustive, but will give you some idea of the life that surrounds you here. For more detail, an excellent reference is Frederic Steele's *At Timberline: A Nature Guide to the Mountains of the Northeast*, published by the Appalachian Mountain Club, Boston, Massachusetts and available through the Appalachian Trail Conference.

Your welcome to Maine may well be the excited chatter of the **red squirrel** (*Tamiasciurus hudsonicus*), a hyperactive little mammal that takes strong exception to any intrusion on its turf and will not hesitate to lighten unguarded food supplies. This is the only squirrel that you will see along the Trail in Maine. Through the dark coniferous forests of the Mahoosucs, you may be lucky enough to glimpse the red squirrel's nemesis, the rare and elusive **pine marten** (*Martes americana*). Both animals find shelter in the spruce-fir forest that dominates much of Maine and supports an important part of the state's forest industry. The prolific **balsam fir** (*Abies balsamea*) is the favorite Christmas tree of the region. The heady incense of drying balsam bough beds once spiced the dreams of shelter users along the Trail in Maine. The high-altitude acidic bogs of the Mahoosucs contain many interesting plants, but the foundation of these huge natural sponges is **peat moss** (*Sphagnum spp.*).

North of the East B Hill Road, the Trail climbs gently through a mixed forest. In May, the Trail is carpeted with the straw-colored bells of the **wild oat** (*Uvularia sessilifolia*), the dappled leaves and solitary, bright yellow blossom of the **dogtooth violet** (*Erythronium americanum*), and the bright green leaves and multiple yellow blossoms of the **yellow Clintonia** (*Clintonia borealis*). (The blossoms later give way to deep-blue berries. These mildly toxic fruits are *not* "blueberries".) During June, you will find many specimens of the white to pink **lady's slipper** (*Cypripedium acaule*), the purple **common trillium** (*Trillium erectum*), aptly known to locals as "stinking Benjamin", and the lovely white and purple-striped **painted trillium** (*Trillium undulatum*). Here, too, are numerous specimens of the tall **Indian cucumber** (*Medeola virginiana*), identified by two prominent leaf whorls on the otherwise bare stem. Throughout the summer, look for the small, pointed, white petals of the **starflower**, whose Latin name is the wonderfully lilting *Trientalis borealis*.

Passing along the Wyman Mountain ridge line, look for the small, candy-striped blossoms of the **wood sorrel** (*Oxalis montana*), whose leaves carpet the acidic soils of the spruce-fir forest type. (Oxalic acid from crushed wood sorrel leaves readily removes pitch from hands.) Look also for the small white flower of the **goldthread** (*Coptis groenlandica*), whose bitter, bright, yellow-orange root is reputed to be a remedy for mouth sores. Between Wyman and Hall mountains, you will pass through lovely stands of **white birch** (*Betula papyrifera*), also known as paper birch or canoe birch.

In the deep, glacial notch between Hall and Moody Mountains, you may glimpse the **white-tailed deer** (*Odocoileus virginianus*), common in Maine, but living here near the northern limits of its natural range. In the hardwood forest along the gradual descent from Moody Mt. to Black Brook Notch, notice the large old specimens of **yellow birch** (*Betula alleghaniensis*), whose rough, thick bark bears little resemblance to the papery yellow covering of young yellow birch trees. The sandy flood plain near Black Brook supports many specimens of **Indian poke** (*Veratrum viride*), whose large, brilliantly-green, prominently-ribbed leaves are sometimes confused with skunk cabbage.

Descending from the **black spruce** (*Picea mariana*)/balsam fir krummholz ("crooked wood") of the sparsely-wooded summit of Old Blue, you enter the high saddle between that peak and Elephant Mountain. Here, at the col above Clearwater Brook, you stand in a forest of balsam fir and **red spruce** (*Picea rubens*) that has never been harvested by humans. Trees within your sight have been dated back to 1620. For some distance south and north of this point, you pass through a forest that is nearing the end of a natural cycle. Much of the fir was killed from 1976–1985 by an epidemic infestation of the spruce budworm (*Choristoneura fumiferana*), a natural phenomenon that occurs roughly every fifty years. The ancient spruce are deteriorating, and the forest is beginning to break up. The abundant softwood seedlings are ready to respond to the sunlight and begin a new forest cycle. Here, you may well glimpse the rare, **black-backed, three-toed woodpecker** (*Picoides arcticus*), whose specialized diet of bark insects that frequent trees that have been dead for a year or two attracts it to this old forest.

The hardwood bench just above Highway 17 bears an early spring carpet of **spring beauty** (*Claytonia caroliniana*) and dogtooth violet. Here, in the dense spruce-fir forest near

Moxie Pond, you may encounter the gentle, gray **Canada jay** (*Perisoreus canadensis*), also known as the "whiskey jack" or "gorby". In stark contrast to the raucous **bluejay** (*Cyanocitta cristata*), the Canada jay is soft-voiced and intensely curious. The gorby may follow you for some distance through the woods and will always welcome a handout of trail mix. At Sabbath Day Pond Lean-to, your evening may be enriched by the haunting wail of the **common loon** (*Gavia immer*), a symbol of the Maine wild lands that you will encounter throughout your journey to Katahdin. The campsite at Little Swift River Pond offers a good chance for an encounter with the giant of the Maine woods, whose tracks and large, oval, fecal pellets ("mooseltoe") you have seen often along the Trail. The **moose** (*Alces alces*) enjoys feeding on water plants, and the opportunity the water affords to escape the clouds of biting insects that you may also have noticed.

You've just crossed Maine Highway 4, and are following the gravel path of the old highway down towards the Sandy River footbridge. Take a moment to look along the right-hand edge of the Trail and, if it is spring, you'll find the oval green leaves and delicate, white/pink, hyacinth-fragrant flowers of the **mayflower** or "trailing arbutus" (*Epigaea repens*). A bit later in the season, the delicate white spray of the **Canada mayflower** (*Maianthemum canadense*) colors the edges of the footpath. In autumn, the hardwood forest ahead glows with the scarlet leaves of the **red maple** (*Acer rubrum*), the yellow-orange of the **sugar maple** (*Acer saccharum*), and the golden of the gray, smooth-barked **American beech** (*Fagus grandifolia*). Beechnuts, along with the fruit of the **beaked hazelnut** (*Corylus cornuta*) are favorite fall foods of creatures such as the white-striped **eastern chipmunk** (*Tamias striatus*).

The three-mile traverse of Saddleback's alpine garden is a special experience. Shortly after you pass above the stunted balsam fir krummholz at treeline, watch to the left of the Trail for an unusual resident of this alpine zone, an **eastern larch** (*Larix laricina*). This particular patch of this deciduous conifer, whose needles turn brilliant yellow in the fall, forms a large bushy growth adjacent to the footpath. Ahead, the Trail is surrounded by beds of balsam fir and of black spruce, whose accommodation to the harsh climate has been to spread out in large, mattress-like formations only a foot or two in height. The footpath itself, disturbed by decades of hikers' boots, offers an hospitable seedbed for the delicate, white-flowered **Greenland sandwort** (*Arenaria groenlandica*), which blooms throughout the summer.

Near the summit of Saddleback, and further on in the alpine zones of The Horn and Saddleback Jr., June hikers will enjoy the beautiful, small, white flowers of the **diapensia** (*Diapensia lapponica*), protruding from the dense, green, "pincushion" mats of this plant community, whose members appear to crowd together for mutual protection against the climate. Also common are the tiny pink flowers and waxy green leaves of the **mountain cranberry** (*Vaccinium vitis-idaea*), whose bright red berries offer late-summer hikers a tart addition to their larder; the common **blueberry** (*Vaccinium angustifolium*), a delicious addition to cereal or pancakes for August hikers; and the **dwarf bilberry** (*Vaccinium cespitosum*), a low alpine plant whose berries resemble blueberries. In early summer, the white flower clusters of the **Labrador tea** (*Ledum groenlandicum*), a relatively tall plant whose green leaves have a conspicuous rusty wool appearance, mingle with the pink flowers of the **pale laurel** (*Kalmia polifolia*). Across the saddle, islands of sedges are punctuated with the white tufts of **hare's tail** (*Eriophorum spissum*).

On a quiet spring or early summer day, hikers who pause at treeline on the descent down Saddleback Jr. will hear one of the most glorious of all of the sounds of the north woods—the clear, piping whistle of the **white-throated sparrow** (*Zonotrichia albicollis*). As you cross Poplar Ridge, you will find none of the **trembling aspen** (*Populus tremuloides*) or "poplar" for which the ridge is named. This pioneer species has disappeared from the once-fire-scarred ridge as a more shade-tolerant forest has evolved, but you will see many of these trees along the Trail in Maine. Together with its cousins, the **balsam poplar** (*Populus balsamea*), with its large, fragrant, resinous buds, and the **bigtooth aspen** (*Populus grandidentata*), the poplar brightens the autumn forest with golden leaves. Its buds are a favorite food for grouse.

As you pick your way carefully down the Poplar Ridge ledges, notice the delicate, trailing, woody vine, tiny leaves, and small white berry of the **snowberry** (*Gaultheria hispidula*). Some large boulders and ledges support clusters of the evergreen **Christmas fern** (*Polystichum acrostichoides*). Passing through the hardwood forest at the base of Poplar Ridge towards evening, listen for the beautiful, descending warble of the **veery** (*Hylocichla fuscesens*) and the flute-like trill of the **wood thrush (***Hylocichla mustelina***)**. All along the Trail, the three-part compound leaf of the **sarsaparilla** (*Aralia nudicaulis*), spreading horizontally from a bare stem about one-foot high, identifies this plant, whose fleshy root contributed flavoring to a pioneer beverage. Shortly before the last drop to Orbeton Canyon, notice the very large **northern white cedar** (*Thuja canadensis*) beside the Trail.

As you pass through the mixed-wood forest north of Orbeton Stream, the heart-stopping thunder of an escaping **ruffed grouse** (*Bonasa umbellus*), known throughout Maine as the "partridge", may quicken your interest. In the spring, it is common to encounter a pitifully "injured" female grouse, whose broken-wing act lures many predators away from her brood of tiny chicks (who you may see scattering away in the opposite direction). Higher, in the spruce-fir forest along the Abraham–Spaulding–Sugarloaf ridge, you are likely to see the **spruce grouse** (*Canachites canadensis*) or "fool-hen", whose apparent fearlessness stems (at least in part) from years of protected status. Notice the bright red eye patch sported by the males.

The dense spruce-fir forest of this area also shelters the rarely seen **bobcat** (*Lynx rufus*) and the extremely rare (in Maine) **lynx** (*Lynx canadensis*), distinguished from its smaller cousin by prominent ear tufts. Both animals prey on the common **snowshoe hare** (*Lepus americanus)*, which you may see in transition between its white winter and brown summer fur. They may even kill a **porcupine** (*Erethizon dorsatum*), though this prickly mammal is more at risk from the agile **fisher** (*Martes pennanti*), the largest of the weasel family in this region. Night hikers may encounter the **short-tailed weasel** (*Mustela erminea*), out on a hunting expedition.

As you cross the Bigelow Range, hold to the footpath across the small alpine zones of West Peak and Avery Peak. There are some rare plant species here, and even the more common alpine flora will be thankful not to be crushed under your vibrams. As you approach the Flagstaff Road, the trail is fringed by the fast-growing **speckled alder** (*Alnus rugosa*). The early springtime forest here is brightened by the white blossoms of the **serviceberry** (shadbush) tree (*Amelanchier laevis*). Across the shoulder of Roundtop Mountain, the understory of the hardwood forest is thick with **witch hobble** (*Viburnum alnifolium*), whose large clusters of white flowers brighten the early summer forest. (The shrub's name derives from an ancient belief that its twisted, rubbery stems would ensnare any witch who sought to flee through a grove of the plants—an image easily understood by Trail maintainers.) Here, too, are the shrub-like **mountain maple** (*Acer spicatum*) the striking **striped maple** (*Acer pensylvanicum*) or "moosewood", whose large leaves and greenish, striped stems (on young trees) offer easy identification, and the **mountain ash** (*Sorbus americana*), whose bright red berries offer autumn food for birds. A little further on, nearing East Carry Pond, the corridor contains a small portion of a **jack pine** (*Pinus banksiana*) plantation.

The path up the lower portions of Moxie Bald Mountain is lined with Maine's tiny dogwood, the **bunchberry** (*Cornus canadensis*), whose large, white "flowers" (actually petal-like structures that surround the flowers themselves) give way to bright red berries in mid to late summer. This should not be confused with the common **checkerberry** (*Gaultheria procumbens*), whose single, bright red berry and leaves have a pleasant wintergreen flavor. (Be sure to take the North Peak Trail out into an old burn that supports a rich carpet of blueberry plants.)

Down along the rapids of the West Branch of the Piscataquis River (where those enticed by the swimming holes should be wary of the **poison ivy** (*Rhus radicans*) that is common along the banks), several sections of the Trail pass magnificent specimens of old-growth **eastern white pine** (*Pinus strobus*) and **red oak** (*Quercus rubra*). One of the MATC crews that built this trail enjoyed the very rare sight of a Maine **black bear** (*Ursus americanus*). Though common, this creature is extremely shy, and will avoid your notice if at all possible.

Near the Blanchard/Monson town line, you will pass through on old farm field that has been planted with a number of exotic conifers. A natural pioneer that has reclaimed many an old field in Maine is the **white spruce** (*Picea glauca*), whose bluish-green foliage sometimes resembles Colorado blue spruce.

As you descend through the hardwood forest towards Lily Pond, you may notice an unusually large (for this far north) **black cherry** (*Prunus serotina*) tree on the north side of the Trail. More common in Maine are the white-flowered **pin cherry** (*Prunus pensylvanica*) and the **choke cherry** (*Prunus virginiana*). The stick and mud home of the local **beaver** (*Castor canadensis*) will probably be visible on the far shore of the pond. (By this time in your journey you may well have been forced to bushwhack or to follow a new section of the Trail to avoid an area flooded by one of these industrious creatures.)

The slate ledges of Elliotsville support a rich variety of lichens. The aptly named **ring lichen** (*Parmelia centrifuga*) and leathery **rock tripe** (*Umbilicaria hyperborea*) are common. But, the most conspicuous lichens are the extensive mats of **Cladonias**, including the gray, dry, tufted mats of **reindeer lichen** (*Cladonia rangiferina*) and the scarlet-capped rods of the **British soldiers** (*Cladonia cristatella*). Further along the Trail, numerous species of **clubmoss** (*Lycopodium spp.*) carpet the forest floor. Especially prominent in this region are the shining clubmoss (*Lycopodium lucidulum*), the **ground cedar** (*Lycopodium complanatum*) and the **ground pine** (*Lycopodium obscurum*).

On the Barren–Chairback Range, as you navigate the infamous Fourth Mountain Bog, take a moment to examine the fascinating, vase-shaped **pitcher plant** (*Sarracenia purpurea*). The stiff, downward-pointing "mouth" hairs trap insects into the water-filled lower portion of the plant, where they are digested.

What appear to be the tracks of a large dog along the Trail north of Gulf Hagas may well be signs of the **eastern coyote** (*Canis latrans*), a recent Maine resident that has become increasingly common over the past 15 years. Traveling up along Gulf Hagas Brook you will pass (in addition to large white pine) some fine old **eastern hemlock** (*Tsuga canadensis*). This lovely conifer, graced with one of the most delicate twig structures of any tree, once provided most of the tanning bark for the Northeast's leather-goods industries. Along the forest floor, notice the ghostly **Indian pipe** (*Monotropa uniflora*), whose lack of color reveals its lack of chlorophyll and its saprophytic reliance on decaying vegetation for nourishment. In spring, the bog south of the Carl Newhall Lean-to glows with the pink blossoms of the **rhodora** (*Rhododendron canadense*).Quantities of late-summer **raspberries** (*Rubus idaeus*) may be found in the old cut-over areas just east of the Trail corridor. The summit of Gulf Hagas Mountain offers a formidable **blackberry** (*Rubus canadensis*) "jungle".

Along the shore of Mud Pond, you will pass through a lovely stand of **red pine** (*Pinus resinosa*), also known as "Norway pine", not because it is an exotic, but because of its early association with the village of Norway, Maine. You have passed isolated red pine specimens throughout your journey across Maine, and will be surrounded by red pine if you camp at Antlers tonight, but this stand is the most extensive in the Trail corridor. The open forest here is rich with mosses, ferns, and ericaceous plants.

North of Nahmakanta Lake, the Trail along Pollywog Gorge passes a number of large white pine, and isolated red pine. Don't look for them, because they are rare and fragile, but your surroundings in the gorge also contain the **fragrant fern** (*Dryopteris fragrans*) and the even more uncommon **luminous moss** (*Schistostega pennata*).

The trees, shrubs, and mosses that have by now become familiar companions grace your path along the Rainbow Ledges, but the crimson leaves of the autumn blueberry plants underscore the area's name. Along the lowlands east of Hurd Brook, early on a fall evening, the long-billed **woodcock** (*Philohela minor*) may betray its excellent camouflage by taking sudden flight, a startling vertical "leap" of perhaps ten feet, a brief hover, then a rapid departure. **Woodpeckers** are common here: the small **downy** (*Dendrocopus pubescens*) and the somewhat larger **hairy** (*Den-drocopus villosus*). The loud, rather maniacal staccato call of the **pileated woodpecker** (*Dryocopus pileatus*) alerts you to the presence of this large bird. Even when the forest seems quiet, if you pause for long you may well be surrounded by the querulous squeaking chirp or namesake "chick-a-dee-dee" of a flock of the small, friendly, inquisitive, **black-capped chickadee** (*Parus atricapillus*).

The plant and animal riches of the Appalachian Trail in Maine continue to unfold as you travel the last few miles of the Trail. From the mixed woods of the Nesowadnehunk to the conifers of the Hunt Trail, the diversity of life that has accompanied your journey continues to delight your senses. The huge arctic-alpine zone of Katahdin supports most of the boreal species that you encountered on mountains further south in Maine. Fittingly, this magnificent monolith also shelters a species found nowhere else on earth: the relict **Katahdin butterfly** (*Oeneis polixenes katahdin*). Shelter these wonders in your memories until you once again are fortunate enough to experience the Appalachian Trail in Maine.

3

The Appalachian Trail
Maine to Georgia

The Appalachian National Scenic Trail is a continuous, marked footpath extending through the mountain lands of the eastern Atlantic states. It extends more than 2,100 miles from Katahdin, a massive granite monolith in the central Maine forest, to Springer Mountain in northern Georgia. Developed initially in the 1920s and 30s as an amateur recreational project, the Trail extending along the crest of the Appalachian Mountains has evolved to become a linear National Park.

The Appalachian Trail traverses fourteen states. Virginia has the longest section with approximately 25% of total Trail mileage; Maine has roughly 13% of total Trail mileage. West Virginia has the shortest section with ten miles along the Virginia–West Virginia boundary just below the Potomac River at Harpers Ferry. The greatest elevation along the Trail route is Clingman's Dome in the Great Smokies at 6,642 feet. At its lowest elevation, the Trail is only slightly above sea level where it crosses the Hudson River. Some 900 miles of the 2,100 mile route are within eight National Forests and two National Parks.

The Appalachian Trail was first proposed in 1921 by regional planner, forester, author, and philosopher, Benton MacKaye of Shirley, Massachusetts. From his journeys in the New England mountains, MacKaye conceived the idea of a trail which would be an endless skyline wild area. He gave expression to this plan in an article entitled "The Appalachian Trail, An Experiment in Regional Planning" which was published in the October, 1921 issue of the *Journal Of American Institute Of Architects*.

Others had proposed extensive through trails in the New England region but the concept of a super trail along the Appalachian ranges was primarily MacKaye's. The publication of MacKaye's proposal aroused considerable interest. The clubs in the New York City area were the first to translate this interest into actual new trail construction. In 1922 the first section of The Appalachian Trail was constructed in the Bear Mountain area of the Palisades Interstate Park by clubs affiliated in what later became the New York–New Jersey Trail Conference. Interest in the undertaking soon spread to New England and Pennsylvania. Early enthusiasm, however, died out before much actual field work began.

In 1925, Benton MacKaye and his supporters incorporated the Appalachian Trail Conference (ATC) whose primary purpose was to organize a group to oversee the construction of the entire Appalachian Trail (at that time envisioned as running 1,700 miles from Mt. Washington in N.H. to Cohutta Mountain in Georgia). This early ATC consisted of a federation of the 5 clubs active in trail building and representatives of several agencies, including the U.S. Forest Service and National Park Service.

When this project was first undertaken, all of the Eastern U.S. outdoor organizations involved were confined to the New England and New York areas. There were four existing trail systems which could be incorporated into this super-trail. First, there were the splendidly-maintained Appalachian Mountain Club trails in the White Mountains of New Hampshire. In Vermont, the lower 100 miles of the rapidly developing "Long Trail" were utilized. Between the White and Green Mountains was the Dartmouth Outing Club trail system. In New York there were the comparatively narrow Bear Mountain and Harriman sections of the Palisades Interstate Park. In all, there were perhaps 350 miles out of the envisioned 1,700 miles.

In addition to the four existing northeastern sections, the Trail route through the South could be located in National Forests. Unfortunately, the connected skyline trails were later developed to become the Skyline Drive and the Blue Ridge Parkway, necessitating significant relocations of the A.T. through Virginia.

In 1926, Arthur Perkins, a retired lawyer from Hartford, Connecticut, undertook the task of translating the concept of an endless trail into reality. From his position on the ATC executive committee, he interested various groups in the task of locating and cutting the footpath — which by now had been discussed for five years. Much of the credit for the completion of the Trail project is due to the enthusiasm and momentum developed by Mr. Perkins.

Mr. Perkins was responsible for recruiting Myron H. Avery of Lubec, Maine, and Washington, D.C., to the A.T. project. As Chairman of the Appalachian Trail Conference from 1931 to 1952, Myron H. Avery enlisted the aid and coordinated the work of hundreds of people up and down the East Coast. As late as 1933, Mt. Washington in the Presidentials of N.H. was being seriously considered as the northern terminus of the A.T. By 1934, 1,900 miles of Trail were completed. In 1935, Mr. Avery spearheaded the formation of the Maine Appalachian Trail Club to construct and manage the trail in Maine. This ensured that the northern terminus of the Trail would be on Katahdin in his native state of Maine.

Under the leadership of Myron Avery, the A.T. was first linked from Maine to Georgia in the summer of 1937, when a Civilian Conservation Corps crew constructed the "missing link," a two mile section between Spaulding and Sugarloaf mountains in western Maine. Even though the Trail was now complete, natural disasters, encroaching development, logging pressures, and the impact of the Second World War made it difficult to preserve the Trail as a connected route.

As completion of the Trail neared, considerable thought was given to the formation of a program for the future protection and preservation of the route.

At the Eighth Appalachian Trail Conference held in June, 1937, in the Great Smoky Mountains National Park, Trail

Conference member Edward B. Ballard proposed a plan for providing an insulation zone along the route of the Trail as a region set apart and dedicated to the interest of those who travel on foot. This plan was adopted by the Conference and steps were taken to implement a long-range program to ensure the perpetuation and protection of the Trail. These efforts culminated in the execution of an agreement between the National Park Service and the United States Forest Service on October 15, 1938. Thus was created a new type of recreational area to be known as "The Appalachian Trailway," a zone extending through the National Parks and National Forests for a distance of one mile on each side of the A.T. The A.T. agreement called for a zone in which there was to be no new paralleling road for motor transportation or any other development incompatible with the existence of this area. The agreement further stated that, where possible, the A.T. would be relocated to meet these criteria. A system of lean-tos and simple shelters was also proposed. The Appalachian Trailway Agreement applied to the following regions: the White Mountain National Forest in New Hampshire, the Green Mountain National Forest in Vermont, the Shenandoah National Park, the George Washington and Jefferson National Forests in Virginia, the Blue Ridge Parkway, the Great Smoky Mountains National Park, the Cherokee National Forests in Tennessee, the Pisgah and Nantahala National Forests in North Carolina, and the Chattahoochee National Forest in Georgia.

Similar agreements were later executed between the Appalachian Trail Conference and several states, except that the protected Trailway zone on state-owned land was to be but 1/4 mile, due to the small area of many state parks and reservations.

Protection of the Appalachian Trail was expanded under the National Trails System Act of 1968. As initial components, the Appalachian Trail and the Pacific Crest Trail were designated National Scenic Trails. The Act provides that The Secretary of the Interior, in consultation with the Secretary of Agriculture, will administer the footpath known as the Appalachian Trail, and protect the Trail against incompatible activities and the use of motorized vehicles. Provision was also made for acquisitions of rights-of-way for the Trail both inside and outside the boundaries of federally administered areas, by easement, purchase, exchange, or, as a last resort, by condemnation.

In 1970, the Act was implemented by supplemental agreements among the National Park Service, the U.S. Forest Service, and the Appalachian Trail Conference. These agreements established the specific responsibilities of these three organizations for the initial mapping, selection of rights-of-way, relocations, maintenance, development, acquisition of land, and protection of the Trail. Agreements were also established between the National Park Service and the various states traversed by the Trail. These Agreements encourage states to acquire and protect the right-of-way for the Trail outside of federally owned land.

Slow progress of federal protection efforts and the lack of initiative by some states led Congress in 1978 to amend the National Trails System Act. The amendment, referred to as the Appalachian Trail Bill, represented the collective efforts of a dedicated group of volunteers, federal officials, and concerned citizens. President Carter signed the legislation on March 21, 1978.

The new legislation left the purpose of the original Act unchanged, but emphasized the need to proceed with the protection of the Appalachian Trail by including the acquisition of a trail corridor. Congress authorized an expenditure of 90 million dollars and established a three-year deadline for the completion of a substantial portion of the protection program. The amendment further required that certain plans and progress reports be prepared and submitted for congressional review.

The program continues to be implemented as a combined effort of the National Park Service and the Trail Clubs under the leadership of the Appalachian Trail Conference, with the aid and cooperation of various state and local agencies. In several states, similar programs are progressing concurrently with the federal program.

Through an historic agreement, dated January 26, 1984, and renewed periodically, the National Park Service (NPS) delegated to the ATC the responsibility for the management of lands acquired by the National Park Service for protection of the Appalachian Trail. Assuming the management of the Trail, the ATC works closely with the thirty two local maintaining clubs in order to manage and maintain the Appalachian Trail. In Maine, the ATC has directly delegated the responsibility for management of NPS Trail lands to the Maine Appalachian Trail Club.

As an oversight organization, the ATC is governed by six representatives from each of three regions who serve as the ATC Board of Managers. The Board's officers include a Chairman, a Vice Chairman for each region, a Treasurer, Secretary, and Corresponding Secretary. General meetings of the Appalachian Trail Conference membership are held every two years. The membership of the Trail Conference consists of organizations and individuals who share a commitment to the A.T. by maintaining sections of the Trail or contributing to the Trail project in other ways. The Conference is essentially a volunteer organization.

Suggested Reading

Campfires Along the Appalachian Trail, by Raymond Baker, New York, Carlton Press, 1971. 120p.

The Appalachian Trail, by Ronald M. Fisher, Washington, National Geographic Society, 1972. 199p.

Appalachian Trail Conference Member Handbook, available from the Appalachian Trail Conference, P.O. Box 807, Harpers Ferry, WV 25425. 112p.

4

Development of the Appalachian Trail in Maine

By 1933 the development of the Appalachian Trail was well underway in most areas of the Appalachian Mountains except in Northern New England. A trail through Maine would have to traverse a remote region, giving rise to difficult access and maintenance problems. For a while it was thought that the northern terminus of the A.T. should be at Mount Washington in New Hampshire rather than at Katahdin near Millinocket, Maine.

After a two-year survey of possible routes, a feasible location for the Maine section was developed utilizing existing trails and tote roads. The proposed route appears in an article, "Maine and The Appalachian Trail" by Myron Avery, in the 1933 issue of *In the Maine Woods* (Bangor & Aroostook Railroad, Bangor, Maine).

While many of Myron Avery's achievements are noted elsewhere in this Guide, his efforts in establishing the route of the A.T. in Maine are legendary. It was Mr. Avery who originally galvanized the interest of many of the active trail volunteers during this time. He arranged for most of the Civilian Conservation Corps (CCC) work, determined the locations of campsites, measured the original 269 miles, and wrote the Trail data. He contributed to Trail maintenance each year as either Overseer of Lands or President of the MATC from its formation in 1935 to his death in 1951 at age 52.

The original route of the trail in Maine was influenced by both a 1933 amendment to the *Maine Guide Law* and the location of public accommodations (sporting camps) available along the route. The Maine Guide Law prohibited non-residents from kindling fires in any unorganized township while engaged in camping, hunting or fishing from May 1 to November 30 unless they were at a public campsite or were accompanied by a registered Maine guide. Working out a route for the A.T. included linking existing sporting camps with newly built lean-tos and campsites. Today, only remnants of the extensive network of sporting camps remain. A chain of 40 lean-tos and campsites provide accommodations along the Trail.

Much of the original Appalachian Trail in Maine was designed and built in haste, at a time when manpower limitations and a desire to push the Trail through to Katahdin left little alternative to such an approach. Accordingly, much of the Trail followed old, temporarily abandoned logging roads and low terrain, bypassing many of the attractive natural features for which the A.T. is so well known today.

In 1933, Walter D. Greene, Broadway actor, Maine guide and later President of the MATC, almost single-handedly scouted and marked the trail over the difficult Barren–Chairback Range. Later in the same year, W. D. Greene, M. H. Avery, and other volunteers marked 77 miles of trail from Katahdin to the Pleasant River, thus completing a trail from Katahdin to the Piscataquis River, a total of 118 miles. In September 1933, 52 miles of the Trail from Blanchard to Bigelow Mountain were marked by S. S. Philbrook and others. Game Warden Helon N. Taylor continued the Trail along the crest of the Bigelow Range to The Horns Pond and opened the seven-mile long Bigelow Range Trail to Stratton. In the following year he completed the main trail to Sugarloaf Mountain. Other groups active at this time included the Maine Forest Service and the State Department of Inland Fisheries and Game. In the Barren–Chairback Range, local sporting camp owners Ralph E. York and W. M. Dore cut new side trails from their respective camps to the Appalachian Trail.

During 1934, the existing Trail was further improved and side trails were cut to Jo-Mary Mountain and Gulf Hagas. Professor

N. H. Sawyer, Jr., with a party from the Bates College Outing Club, made an extensive survey for the route of the uncompleted Trail between Grafton Notch and Saddleback Mountain.

In 1935, the Appalachian Trail in Maine was officially adopted as a project in the Civilian Conservation Corps (CCC) program. Crews were sent out from the CCC Camps at Millinocket, Greenville, Flagstaff, and Rangeley. All of the existing Trail was improved in 1935 with the exception of two sections, from the Kennebec River to Blanchard, and from the East Branch of the Pleasant River to Nahmakanta Lake. The precise trail route, between Maine Highway 4 and Grafton Notch, was completed by C. Granville Reed of the CCC. The Flagstaff CCC group scouted out a section which they called "the Arnold Trail," between Pierce Pond and Bigelow Mountain via the Carry Ponds. The Rangeley CCC group opened the new trail from Saddleback Mountain to the Andover–South Arm Road, a distance of 27 miles. By year's end, seven lean-tos had been built by the CCC.

The Flagstaff and Millinocket CCC Camps were closed at the end of 1935. The uncompleted Trail work was undertaken the following year by two crews from the Rangeley CCC Camp. One crew, under the direction of George Winter, Jr., completed the Trail between Grafton Notch and the Andover–South Arm Road. They built the Squirrel Rock, Frye Brook and Grafton Notch Lean-tos, developed a side trail to Table Rock above Grafton Notch and completed the section of Trail between the Saddleback and Sugarloaf Ranges.

A second crew from the Rangeley CCC Camp completed a short section on Roundtop Mountain, cut the remainder of "the Arnold Trail" Route on Little Bigelow Mountain, built two lean-tos at Horns Pond on Bigelow and nearly completed the Trail west from Sugarloaf to Orbeton Stream.

During 1936, a group from the Greenville CCC Camp improved the Trail between Nahmakanta Stream and the East Branch of the Pleasant River. They made further improvements on Moxie Bald Mountain and the section between the Kennebec River and Blanchard. The side trail system in Gulf

Hagas was improved the same summer by opening the route along the rim of the West Branch of the Pleasant River.

Trail work for 1937 was continued by CCC crews from the Bridgton and Greenville Camps. They built two additional lean-tos and recleared the entire route. On August 14, 1937, the final link in the entire Appalachian Trail was completed on the north slope of Spaulding Mountain. This "original route" included four canoe ferries in Maine, the West Branch of the Penobscot River, Rainbow Lake, the Kennebec River, and Moxie Pond.

In 1938, the Bridgton CCC crew built four additional lean-tos: Spaulding Mountain, Jerome Brook, East Carry Pond and Pierce Pond. A crew from the Greenville Camp completed a lean-to on the east slope of Moxie Bald Mountain.

During 1939, crews from a Forest Service Camp on the Andover–B Hill Road and the Jefferson CCC Camp went over the Trail from Maine Highway 16 to the Maine–New Hampshire line to reopen the route and eliminate the damage caused by the New England hurricane of September, 1938.

During the 1940s, the condition of the Trail seriously deteriorated due to hurricanes, newly mechanized logging operations, and the need for trail maintainers to fulfill their military obligations.

Following World War II, the Maine Appalachian Trail Club ex-panded its activities to restore the Trail. In 1950, the Trail was re-located over the Barren–Chairback Range. Helon Taylor relocated the Trail where it had been obliterated by the flowage of the newly formed Flagstaff Lake (1949–1950). In 1956, he also relocated 10 miles of Trail between the West Branch of the Penobscot and Rainbow Ledges following the 1955 collapse of the old cable foot bridge across the West Branch. In 1958 there were relocations on Bemis Mountain and at the foot of Moxie Pond.

In the late 1950s, the Club completed the chain of lean-tos across Maine. No lean-tos had been constructed since the CCC ended their program in 1938, twenty years previously. Under the outstanding leadership of MATC President Louis Chorzempa and Shelter Chairman Carl Newhall, the Club completed the chain, constructing no fewer than 17 new lean-tos of logs and corrugated aluminum roofing.

A major program of relocation to improve the route of the A.T. in Maine began with the passage of the National Trails System Act in 1968. At that time, the Maine Appalachian Trail Club reviewed the location of the entire Trail in the state. This review, and subsequent planning, led to a new trail construction program relocating over 180 miles — more than half of the Trail in Maine. The goal was to relocate the A.T. to a route more rewarding to the hiker, harmonious with landowners, and which could be effectively managed. Under the leadership of David Field (President from 1976–1986 and Overseer of Lands from 1987–1994), the relocation program continued through the 1970s and the 1980s, as the Club worked with private landowners and State and Federal agencies to secure a permanent protected location for the Appalachian Trail in Maine.

Some of the major relocation projects were:

1974	14 miles between Bigelow and Crocker
1975	23 miles in White Cap–Gulf Hagas and Little Swift River Pond areas
1979	12 miles C-Pond relocation
1981	23 miles Nesuntabunt Mountain and Dunn Notch
1982	27 miles Rainbow Stream and Little Boardman
1983	Rainbow flowage, White Cap, Carry Ponds, and Safford Notch
1986	17 miles at Gulf Hagas Brook, Lily Pond, Pierce Pond Stream, Little Bigelow and Lone Mountain
1987	16 mile Elliotsville relocation
	7.6 mile Blanchard relocation
	4.7 mile Pleasant Pond Mountain
	1.7 mile Mt. Abraham side trail
1989	5 miles near Monson
	6 miles Holly Brook
1992	Bemis Stream side trail relocation

Further plans are to continue relocations as necessary within the newly surveyed corridor and to begin to concentrate on improvements to pathway hardening and stabilization.

The relocation program forced the abandonment of eleven campsites or lean-tos. Twenty-eight new or replacement lean-tos have been completed since 1970. Another half dozen locations are being considered for addition or replacement. A program of sanitary facility improvement began in 1973, with 40 new privies having been completed since then.

With the completion of the relocation and campsite development work, the MATC has turned attention to the growing need for footpath rehabilitation and erosion control. Efforts along these lines were greatly aided between 1978 and 1989 by the volunteer work of Student Conservation Association (SCA) crews under the leadership of MATC Overseer, Jim Mitchell. Those crews were particularly active in the Bigelow Preserve, Sawyer Notch, and Blanchard. From 1986 through 1989, SCA work was supplemented by youths from the Maine Conservation Corps (MCC).

Since 1991, the Club has supported its own volunteer Trail crew. Known as the FORCE, the Footpath Recovery Crew is a group of adults and youths from throughout the U.S. who spend a week or more at a time on trail work under the direction of experienced trail crew leaders.

Increasing Trail use also finds the Club directly involved in educational activities designed to mitigate the impact of hikers on fragile ecological areas. One example is the volunteer caretaker program at Bigelow Col. The MATC is working cooperatively with other public agencies and private organizations to provide caretakers for other heavily used locations.

For an account of the historical background of the regions traversed by the Maine A.T. from Katahdin to the Maine–New Hampshire border, refer to Chapter 2 "Along the Appalachian Trail in Maine" by Myron Avery in the 1953 edition of *The Guide to the Appalachian Trail in Maine*. Reprints are available from the Appalachian Trail Conference, Box 807, Harpers Ferry, WV 25425.

5

Management of the Trail in Maine

The Appalachian Trail is a unique public footpath extending through 14 states. Its route will be protected along the entire length by federal or state ownership of the land itself or by rights-of-way. From inception, Trail construction and management has been a cooperative venture between the Appalachian Trail Conference, local volunteer organizations, the National Park Service, the U.S. Forest Service and many other agencies within each state. The sheer number of organizations involved in the management of the Trail from Maine to Georgia defies the imagination, but the passion and commitment of volunteers and workers of the Appalachian Trail community provides the living stewardship vital to preserving and enhancing the A.T.

The Maine Appalachian Trail Club

The Maine Appalachian Trail Club (MATC) is an all volunteer, public service organization that was formed in 1935 to assume responsibility for management, maintenance and protection of the Appalachian Trail in Maine. It maintains the A.T. from Katahdin to Maine Highway 26 in Grafton Notch (267 miles) and over 40 miles of related side trails. The 14 miles of the A.T. between Grafton Notch and the Maine–New Hampshire state line, located primarily on the Mahoosuc Trail, are maintained by the Appalachian Mountain Club (AMC). The MATC is not a hiking or an outing club. It exists solely for the protection and perpetuation of the A.T. In 1995, the MATC reported 19,883 volunteer hours devoted to the Trail in Maine.

The Maine Appalachian Trail Club organization is governed by a slate of elected officers and Board of Directors chosen every other year at the Club's annual meeting in April. These officers and directors organize and coordinate the Club's general business, work trips and trail management of over 35,000 acres of land in the Maine Trail Corridor.

The MATC works to keep the Trail an unspoiled natural wilderness footpath on the most scenic and challenging terrain, so that hikers may enjoy the best possible hiking experience. Club members take pride in maintaining the Trail to the highest standards possible through group work trips and the work of individual maintainers. From late April to early October, club members clear blowdowns, clip brush, paint blazes, update and repair signs, and carefully monitor the Trail and its environment. The Club also runs a series of larger group trips to handle major projects such as cutting new trail, building or repairing lean-tos, constructing rock steps, installing water bars, or building bog bridges. These work trips provide an excellent learning experience for both the new member and some "old hands". More help is always welcome.

In 1991, the Club also organized a Footpath Recovery Crew (FORCE) to tackle the most substantial maintenance tasks. Each summer, volunteers from other parts of the country join with MATC members to work on the Trail. Directed by experienced crew leaders, volunteers receive food and lodging at a base camp in exchange for their labor. The FORCE program's multiple goals are (1) to teach and accomplish quality treadway construction and repair on the A.T. in Maine; (2) to supplement the ongoing efforts of maintainers and volunteers on the A.T. in Maine; and (3) to improve and build the trail-repair skills of the crew participants and MATC volunteers.

General maintenance of the A.T. in Maine is assigned by the MATC to interested groups and individuals, who become members of the club. Numbering 90 in 1996, these assignments form the backbone of Trail maintenance in Maine. The respective responsibilities of the Club and these "local maintainers" is spelled out in formal maintenance agreements. At the present time, there are three types of assignments: trail maintenance, lean-to and campsite maintenance, and corridor monitoring.

Trail maintenance includes the removal of obstructions (such as trees which have blown down) and other vegetation from the pathway, renewal of paint blazes, repair of rock cairns, and installation of signs, all according to maintenance standards published by the MATC. The length of a maintenance section varies from two to over eight miles depending on the size of the group involved. The Club retains overall responsibility for the maintenance and management of the Trail, oversees the work of the maintainer, and represents the maintainer in all contacts with landowners, public agencies and the Appalachian Trail Conference. Trail location, the construction of campsites, shelters, sanitary facilities, bridges, and heavy footpath construction are beyond the scope of the individual maintainer and are MATC responsibilities.

Lean-to and campsite maintenance includes regular inspection and general upkeep of shelters and campsite areas. Regular monitoring and maintenance extends the longevity of existing structures.

Corridor boundary maintenance is a relatively new responsibility related to the need to regularly monitor the boundary of National Park land holdings and rights of way for encroachments, timber trespass or other forms of incompatible use. Corridor monitors address the need to manage the lands within the A.T. corridor beyond the actual footpath itself.

Although a few existing maintenance assignments were made over 50 years ago, new maintenance assignments do become available from time to time. Interested volunteers should contact the MATC for more information.

In addition to the local maintainers, the club has about 500 members who pay annual dues, hold voting rights, and are active in many Club tasks such as sign construction or guidebook editing that do not involve a formal trail assignment. These members often turn out to assist with trail work not expected of regular maintainers. Whether it is an individual maintainer spending a day clipping brush along the Trail or an extended effort by a larger group to build a new lean-to, Club members share a sense of accomplishment, camaraderie, pride, and a commitment to the preservation and protection of the Trail. The MATC always welcomes new members. A membership application is included in the front of this guidebook.

Trail Administrative Agencies and Relationships

Administrative responsibility for the Appalachian Trail in Maine changed with the passage of the National Trails System Act of 1968. The National Park Service (NPS) holds the primary responsibility for the acquisition, development, and administration of the entire A.T. In January, 1984, the Park Service signed an historic agreement with the Appalachian Trail Conference (ATC), whereby the authority for the management of the A.T. was delegated to the ATC. The Appalachian Trail Conference coordinates planning and management of the A.T. through: (1) the assignment of responsibility for sections of the A.T. to major maintaining organizations, (2) the development and publication of Trail standards, (3) the development of Trail management policies, and (4) serving as a liaison between the volunteer Trail organizations and the National Park Service. Management authority has since been transferred to the MATC for lands in Maine that are owned by the NPS.

The MATC, the ATC, the NPS, and the Maine Bureau of Parks and Recreation are pursuing a program for the protection of the A.T. in Maine that includes the acquisition of fee and easement property rights to the footpath and the associated variable-width land corridor. When the protection program has been completed, about 185 miles of the A.T. in Maine will be owned by the National Park Service, with about 95 miles held by the State of Maine (Bureau of Parks and Lands, Baxter State Park, and Department of Inland Fisheries and Wildlife). By the end of 1995, all but about three miles of the A.T. in Maine was located on publicly-owned lands. Only one-half mile of the

Trail coincides with a public road — the Perimeter Road in Baxter State Park.

Lands outside the A.T. corridor will continue to be held by private owners. Most of the private lands along the corridor in Maine are held in large parcels (often entire townships) by forest-products corporations and the heirs of old family estates. (Before public acquisition of the corridor, seventy percent of the Trail in Maine was owned by eight companies and the clients of one land-management firm.) This land ownership pattern, with its focus on timber management, has contributed greatly to the retention of the relatively wild character of the lands along the Trail.

Although the Trail crosses lands owned by several State agencies, the Maine Bureau of Parks and Lands (Department of Conservation) is the lead organization for the state's involvement in the protection and management of the Appalachian Trail. The Maine State Trails System Act of 1973 directed the Bureau to establish a Maine Trails System, and to include the Appalachian Trail as a "primitive trail" in a manner consistent with the National Trails System Act. The 1973 Act authorized the State to acquire fee or lesser interests along the trails to protect them from incompatible developments, and authorized the Bureau to adopt rules and regulations for the A.T. and other trails that are components of the Maine trail system.

Responsibility for the maintenance and management of the A.T. across the State owned lands, has been delegated to the MATC. The MATC maintains the A.T. in Baxter State Park through an agreement with park supervisors.

The Trail and its management may be either complicated or simplified by the type of land ownership through which the route passes. Even after the protection corridor has been completed, the pathway will continue to pass through the vast commercial forest which has always been the dominant feature of its surroundings. Hikers will continue to see timber harvesting and the logging roads that on one hand disturb the wild character of the Trail, and, on the other, ease access to it for hikers and maintainers alike. No commercial timber harvesting will be allowed on National Park Service land, but the State owned lands are not so restricted. The State agency which manages most of the State owned lands along the Trail is the Maine Bureau of Parks and Lands (Department of Conservation). Much of the Bureau's domain is commercial forest land, owned by the public but managed primarily for timber production. This agency has designated a 1000 foot special management zone along the A.T. Other public management entities along the A.T. include the strict wilderness management program of Baxter State Park (not part of the regular State park system) and wildlife preserves of the Department of Inland Fisheries and Wildlife. Special management plans apply to the various "management units" along the Trail.

Most of the Appalachian Trail in Maine is located in unorganized townships with few residents and no local government. These areas, mostly under corporate ownership, are governed by the State. Land use there is controlled by the Land Use Regulation Commission (Department of Conservation). The LURC operates under a Comprehensive Land Use Plan and a set of rules and regulations designed to meet standards for the use of air, lands, and waters in the State's unorganized territories. The Appalachian Trail itself is zoned by the Commission as a 200-foot wide "primitive recreation corridor" within which development and timber activities are restricted (but not altogether prohibited). In many areas, restrictive zones overlap the Trail affording it and its surroundings varying degrees of additional protection.

The Maine Forest Service (Department of Conservation) has statutory authority for the prevention and suppression of forest fires along most of the A.T. in Maine. Campsite fireplaces must be approved by this agency, which strictly enforces the State's fire laws. The Department of Inland Fisheries and Wildlife enforces Maine hunting, inland fishing, and trapping laws. Its Warden Service, assisted by the Maine Forest Service and qualified private organizations, is responsible for search and rescue along the A.T. outside of Baxter State Park.

The Department of Environmental Protection has responsibility for monitoring activities along the Trail that impact air and overall water quality, and for the enforcement of laws to protect those resources. The Department of Human Services establishes and enforces standards for the disposal of human wastes. The Maine State Police and the several county sheriff departments enforce criminal laws other than those involving forest fire and fish and game laws.

Coordinating the management of the A.T. with all of these diverse public agencies is a real challenge. Working in this complex matrix of public and volunteer organizations requires skills and techniques which were not part of the Trail project in the past. The successful integration of public and volunteer resources in managing and maintaining the Appalachian Trail distinguishes it from other trail systems. A key part of the project in the future is to carry out the stewardship of the Trail while maintaining and enhancing the viability and vitality of the volunteer effort.

6
Trail Synopsis

This chapter is subdivided into seven parts, one for each map, to assist with trip planning. Each division includes:

- Location
- Section information
- Length
- Hiking time
- Elevation gain
- Lean-tos and campsites
- Major peaks
- Trail overview (described north to south)
- Road access
- Supply points, accommodations, and mail drops
- Side trails
- Points of interest
- References and suggested reading

The trail descriptions on the back of each map use a cross reference symbol, *(P)*, indicating that additional historical, geological, or natural history information is found under "points of interest" in this chapter.

A summary of map data appears in a table at the end of this chapter on page 155.

MAP 1
Katahdin to the South End of Nahmakanta Lake

MAP

1

Location
North central Maine, approximately 20 miles west northwest of Millinocket.

Section Information

Section 1: Katahdin to Abol Bridge on West Branch of Penobscot River

Section 2: Abol Bridge to South end of Nahmakanta Lake

	Section 1	Section 2	Map Total
Length	15.1 mi.	25.7 mi.	40.8 mi.
Hiking Time	2 days	2–3 days	4–5 days
Elevation Gain			
Southbound	None	2,200 ft.	2,200 ft.
Northbound	4,600 ft.	2,500 ft.	7,100 ft.
Lean-tos & Campsites	3	4	7
Major Peaks	Katahdin (5,267 ft.)	none	1

Trail Overview

The dominant feature of Section 1 is Katahdin, the highest mountain in Maine and the northern terminus of the Appalachian Trail. The unhindered view of hundreds of lakes, ponds, and lesser peaks set in the vast northern forest of Maine is one of the finest anywhere. The climb to the summit is significant — nearly 5,000 feet in 5 miles with an extensive section above treeline. West of the mountain's base, the A.T. passes three ponds, Tracy, Elbow, and Daicey, before paralleling Nesowadnehunk Stream with its series of scenic waterfalls and quiet pools on the descent toward the West Branch of the Penobscot. The confluence of Nesowadnehunk Stream and the

West Branch of the Penobscot is reached eleven miles south of Katahdin at Pine Point. The Trail follows the Penobscot downstream to the crossing at Abol Bridge. The prominent point in the river visible from the bridge is where Henry David Thoreau camped when he visited this area in the 1840s.

Notable features in this section include: Katahdin and Baxter State Park; Nesowadnehunk Stream and falls; and the West Branch of the Penobscot River.

South of Abol Bridge, the Trail begins a relatively remote stretch ending in Monson 100 miles away. While this portion of the route has been referred to as the "100 Mile Wilderness", it is not true wilderness as the Trail passes through extensive areas of commercial forest where logging has occurred since the early 1800s.

Southbound from Abol Bridge, the path winds easily through the woods, passing Hurd Brook Lean-to before climbing gently over Rainbow Ledges with its excellent views of Katahdin. The A.T. then winds through relatively flat lake country following the shore of Rainbow Lake for over 5 miles, climbs Nesuntabunt Mountain with its views of Katahdin and Nahmakanta Lake, and then follows the shore of Nahmakanta Lake for 2 miles. Nahmakanta, in its wild setting nestled between two mountains, is one of the finest lakes on the entire 2,100 mile Appalachian Trail. Swimming and fishing opportunities abound in this Section.

Section 2 is notable for the undeveloped character of both Rainbow and Nahmakanta Lakes, and the pleasant overlook from Nesuntabunt Mountain. Except at Abol Bridge, access points are limited to long drives over gravel roads.

Road Access

To reach the Katahdin area:

Millinocket is the main access route to the Trail in this area. Mileages to this point by way of Routes I-95, 11 and 157 are:

Boston to Millinocket	306 miles
Portland to Millinocket	203 miles

Katahdin to Nahmakanta Lake

MAP

1

Augusta to Millinocket	146 miles
Bangor to Millinocket	70 miles

From Millinocket, follow signs toward Baxter State Park.

To reach Abol Bridge via the private Golden Road cross to the Golden Road immediately north of the causeway at Millinocket Lake. The Golden Road (toll) allows access through to Greenville (56 miles via Ripogenus Dam and Kokadjo) or to Quebec, Canada, via a system of private logging roads. Cars may be left at Abol Bridge Campground if arrangements are made with the campground owner.

To park near Abol Bridge at the locked gate on the dead-end road outside the Baxter State Park boundary, bear left at a fork in the road about 16 miles from Millinocket. Four miles beyond the fork is the A.T. parking near Abol Bridge. This route does not provide vehicle access to Abol Bridge or points west.

To enter Baxter State Park and reach either Katahdin Stream Campground or Daicey Pond Campground bear right at a fork in the road about 16 miles from Millinocket to reach the Togue Pond Gate at the Park's south entrance. Immediately past the gate, the right fork leads to Roaring Brook Campground and the left fork (the Perimeter Road) leads 8.2 miles to Katahdin Stream Campground or 12 miles to Daicey Pond Campground.

Access for the south end of Section 2 can be made via the Katahdin Iron Works/Jo-Mary Multiple Use Management Forest. The gravel logging roads in this region are private roads open to the public by permit. For information on fees, gate hours, and current road conditions, contact North Maine Woods, P.O. Box 421, Ashland, ME, 04732.

The Jo-Mary Road is the prominent gravel road leaving Maine Highway 11 about 18 miles north of Brownville Junction or 13 miles south of Millinocket. The Jo-Mary Check Point entry gate (fee) provides access to the A.T. at: the south end of Nahmakanta Lake, Nesuntabunt Mountain, or Pollywog Stream. From the gate, it is about 12 miles northwest to the A.T. crossing at Cooper Brook, 24 miles to the south end of Nahmakanta

Lake, 25 miles to Nesuntabunt Mountain, or 27 miles to Polly-wog Stream. Active logging is occurring in this forest. Check with the gatekeeper for directions and current road conditions.

Access to the south end of Section 2 is also possible from Greenville. Go north on the Lily Bay Road through Kokadjo. About 3 miles north of Kokadjo turn right (east) towards Second Roach Pond. Reach a four way intersection in about 5 miles. Turn left (north) and reach the intersection just west of Penobscot Pond in approximately 7 miles. Turn left (north) passing north of Penobscot Pond, reaching the Jo-Mary Road in about 3 miles. Turn left (north) toward Nahmakanta Lake. Take a right turn in about 1 mile for access to the parking area at the south end of Nahmakanta Lake, or continue straight to cross the A.T. near Nesuntabunt Mountain or to reach Pollywog Stream.

Supply Points, Accommodations, and Mail Drops

Millinocket, population 6,500, is the "jumping off place" for all of the A.T. in this area, and is about 20 miles from the Trail. It is the largest town in this part of Maine, and has numerous restaurants, motels, grocery stores, hardware stores, laundro-mats, a hospital, and other medical facilities. The headquarters for Baxter State Park is located in town at 64 Balsam Drive.

There are two private campgrounds on the road between Millinocket and Baxter State Park. Campgrounds operated by Baxter State Park include: Daicey Pond and Katahdin Stream Campgrounds, (both on the Trail); Chimney Pond Camp-ground, (reached by a 3.3 mile hike); and Abol and Roaring Brook Campgrounds. Advance reservations are recom-mended. Abol Campground in Baxter State Park, located off the Perimeter Road, should not be confused with the pri-vately operated campground at Abol Bridge located off the Golden Road.

A modest variety of groceries can be purchased at the small campground store at Abol Bridge where the A.T. crosses the West Branch of the Penobscot River. There are no supply points between Abol Bridge and Monson, 100 miles to the south (Map 3). *Southbound hikers should carry an 8–10 day supply of food. This is the longest remote section along the entire A.T.*

The Post Office ZIP code for Millinocket is 04462.

MAP
1

Side Trails

The Owl Trail (2.2 mi.) The Owl (elev. 3,736 ft.) is a prominent domed peak located on the northwest side of Witherle Ravine. Hunt Spur forms the southeast side of the ravine. The Owl provides excellent views for a moderate climb. Carry water. Leave the A.T. 1.0 mile north of Katahdin Stream Campground. At 0.5 mile cross a tributary of Katahdin Stream, (last water); at 1.8 miles climb more steeply; reach summit at 2.2 miles after leaving the A.T. (or 3.2 miles from Katahdin Stream Campground).

Grassy Pond Trail (1.5 mi.) Grassy Pond is a small pond located west of Katahdin Stream Campground. Relics of an old lumber camp remain on the south shore. The trail leaves the A.T. across the Perimeter Road from Katahdin Stream Campground, passes Grassy Pond, and rejoins the A.T. 0.5 mile north of Daicey Pond. A day hike loop (3.2 miles) visiting Tracy, Elbow, Grassy and Daicey Ponds can be made by combining the A.T. with the Grassy Pond Trail.

Sentinel Mountain Trail (3.2 mi.) Sentinel Mountain (elev. 1,837 ft.) offers an easy hike and unrestricted views of Doubletop, O-J-I, Barren, The Owl, and the entire west flank of Katahdin. Where the A.T. meets Daicey Pond Road, follow Daicey Pond Road north toward Perimeter Road. In 0.1 mile turn west off Daicey Pond Road, and cross Nesowadnehunk Stream. Skirt west side of Kidney Pond. At 0.7 mile reach Sentinel Landing on Kidney Pond. The trail bears southwest away from Kidney Pond and at 1.4 miles crosses Beaver Brook. Trail climbs along stream bed, crossing and re-crossing brook in ravine on northeast side of mountain. Reach ledges at 3.1 miles, summit at 3.2 miles. Trail loops around summit providing views in all directions.

MAP

1

Big and Little Beaver Ponds (0.5 mi.) Trail leaves the A.T. at the east end of Rainbow Lake. Little Beaver Pond is 0.1 mile, and Big Beaver Pond is an additional 0.4 mile.

Rainbow Mountain Trail (1.1 mi.) Leaves the A.T. near Rainbow Lake Camps on the south side of Rainbow Lake. Summit has extensive open areas caused by an old burn and affords good views.

Points of Interest

KATAHDIN The northern terminus of the A.T., Katahdin is one of the Trail's most outstanding features. Focal point of Baxter State Park, the mountain rises as an isolated, massive, gray granite monolith from a central Maine forest that is broken only by the silver sheen of countless lakes. To the Indians it was known as "Kette-Adene" — the "greatest mountain" — and this mountain mass in every way exemplifies the tribute of the age-old name given it by the people who lived under its influence.

From every major direction, Katahdin's aspect is utterly different. It is many mountains. From the south, seen over Togue Pond, approaching from Millinocket, Katahdin is a huge undulating rampart wall. From the east, over Katahdin Lake, it is the rim of a series of broken-open volcanic-like cones. From the north, it is the culminating peak of two parallel ranges which approach the peak from the level lands of the Penobscot East Branch Valley. From the west, it is a long range, overtopping the outlying protecting barrier ranges.

From the summit, on Baxter Peak (5,267 ft.), the surrounding land appears as if a mirror had been broken and scattered over the mantle of the dark green spruce and fir forest cover, with the myriad lakes reflecting the sun's light to the observer. Views from its summit are restricted only by haze and clouds.

Katahdin has been described as an enormous flat fishhook. The projecting point is the rounded dome of Pamola (4,902 ft.). To the Native Americans, Pamola was the deity of Katahdin. In awe of Pamola's wrath, they never dared venture too near Katahdin. Native people who accompanied Charles Turner, Jr. in

1804 told him how Pamola had destroyed an earlier party of Native scouts who had ventured into the fastnesses of Katahdin. At that time no one dared approach the mountain.

In the bend of this fishhook are three enormous basins — Great (South), North, and Little North with sheer gray or pink granite walls arising abruptly almost 2,000 feet above the basin floors. Chimney Pond and Cleftrock Pool are situated in the Great Basin.

Encircling the Great Basin, for three-fourths of its rim, is the famous Knife Edge, a narrow wall of vertically-fractured granite. In places its width is only a few feet, with precipitous slopes dropping 1,500 feet on each side.

Thousands of years ago, the continental glacier planed off the top of this mountain, leaving the flat table land rising toward the south. Later, local glaciers carved out the three basins, leaving the Knife Edge to connect Pamola with the rest of the mountain. The last local glacier disappeared from Katahdin's slopes between ten and fifteen thousand years ago.

The vegetation on Katahdin was also determined by these glaciers. Above treeline at 3,000 feet the flora is similar to that found on the Canadian tundra, in Greenland, and northern Labrador.

In the early days, when Katahdin was truly a remote wilderness peak, even reaching it was difficult. The first recorded ascent of Katahdin is attributed to Charles Turner, Jr. in 1804 who reached the summit via the Hunt Spur, the route now followed by the Appalachian Trail. Explorers such as geologist C. T. Jackson in 1837 and Henry David Thoreau in 1846 came up the West Branch of the Penobscot by bateau and canoe. On his trip, which is recorded in a book titled *Ktaadn*, Thoreau ascended onto the Table Land where he found himself "deep within the hostile ranks of clouds and all objects were obscured by them."

Today, Katahdin is a popular destination for thousands of hikers each year. On a clear day, the views from the mountain are unsurpassed. In foggy or inclement weather, extreme caution is advised as much of the mountain is above treeline.

MAP

1

BAXTER STATE PARK Katahdin lies within Baxter State Park, which was created by gifts from former Governor Percival P. Baxter to the State of Maine in 1931 and subsequent years. Mr. Baxter served five terms in the Maine Legislature and one term as Governor. During these years, he tried to convince his legislative colleagues that this region should be preserved from economic and domestic development. After his governorship, he purchased and donated 5,960 acres including most of Katahdin, forming the nucleus of Baxter State Park in 1931. By the time of his death in 1969, Governor Baxter had purchased and donated to the State some 201,018 acres. The most recent addition to the Park, the purchase of several thousand acres in 1992–93 around Togue Pond, was made possible by funds he left to the Park Authority.

A condition of his gift is that the area shall "forever be used for public park and recreational purposes, shall forever be left in the natural wild state, shall forever be kept as a sanctuary for wild beasts and birds, and that no roads or ways for motor vehicles shall hereafter be constructed therein or hereon." This magnificent gift to the people of Maine stands out as one of the most unusual, generous and foresighted of our country's history. Baxter State Park is the largest acreage east of the Mississippi devoted solely to wilderness uses — recreation is a secondary use.

Baxter State Park is operated by the Baxter State Park Authority. This state agency is charged with maintaining the area as a wilderness preserve and sanctuary and exercises a high degree of control over the number of visitors and their activities. Hikers should obtain a copy of the regulations and become familiar with them before their trip. Be forewarned that the area is at capacity in July, August, and September. Anyone entering the Park, whether by car or on foot, must register at one of the two entry gates or at the nearest campground. Once campground limits are reached, the Park gates are closed. Northbound A.T. hikers entering the Park near Nesowadne-hunk Stream should register at Daicey Pond

Campground, 7.5 miles north of Abol Bridge. Arrangements for accommodations inside the Park should be made in advance whenever possible.

MAP
1

Inquiries should be addressed to:

> Reservation Clerk, Baxter State Park
> 64 Balsam Drive, Millinocket, ME 04462
> Phone: (207) 723-5140

NESOWADNEHUNK STREAM There are many signs of the great log drives along Nesowadnehunk Stream, including Toll Dam and the many stanchions in the rocks which served to anchor the log booms. Stanchions are especially visible at the thundering falls of Little Niagara, Big Niagara and Indian Pitch. Toll Dam, first built in 1879, was used to control water for log drives. The owners of the dam charged a toll for the passage of logs through their "improvements." So rugged was this route, that Hempstead (1931) wrote that "Sourdnahunk logs were recognizable as far as they could be seen. They were distinguished by battered ends, a large number of scars and the absence of bark . . ." The fourth reconstruction of the dam on the original foundation was completed in 1929.

The original A.T. route crossed to the west side of Nesowadnehunk Stream on the Toll Dam, and crossed the West Branch of the Penobscot River on a cable bridge built in 1935–36 by the Patten CCC camps. The bridge failed in the winter of 1948–49 and was rebuilt by the Maine Highway Department in 1950. The circumstance of a large swift river filled with pulpwood made any means other than a bridge for crossing the river difficult at best. Ice and storm damage brought the cable bridge down again in 1955. In 1956–57, the Trail was rerouted down the east side of Nesowadnehunk Stream allowing the West Branch crossing to be made on the then recently built Abol Bridge.

Today, the quiet pools and spectacular falls offer an outstanding hike along what has again become a wilderness stream.

MAP

1

WEST BRANCH OF THE PENOBSCOT RIVER The Penobscot River drainage was one of this region's most important thoroughfares for moving logs in the 1800s. The first large scale river drives began in 1828, and by 1846 there were 250 sawmills above Bangor, where the Penobscot meets the tidewater. Lumber production increased from 2 million board feet in 1846 to 225 million by 1872.

During the winter when all was frozen, the woods were full of lumbermen. They cut and then "yarded" the logs on the ice and banks of streams, whose swollen torrents in early spring carried them to the mills. Oftentimes the drive would be "hung" by low water. Much clearing of streams, removal of obstructions and building of dams was required as men struggled to insure the passage of such uncontrollable craft.

Pine Point marks the confluence of Nesowadnehunk Stream with the West Branch of the Penobscot. Immediately upstream from Pine Point on the West Branch was the proposed site of the "Big A" Dam intended for power generation. Serious opposition caused the project to be abandoned in 1986–87.

Look upstream along the West Branch toward Nesowadnehunk Falls and visualize the story of the river drivers related by Fannie Hardy Eckstorm in her book, *The Penobscot Man*.

On a day in May, during the drive of 1870, two crews of six Penobscot River drivers had just carried their heavy bateaux around the falls and were waiting at the end of the carry for the third boat. The third boat was manned by Big Sebattis Mitchell, a Passamaquoddy, and his bowman, a Penobscot Indian. Attempting the falls was to dare a feat accomplished perhaps but once fully twenty years before. Sebattis persuaded his companion to take the chance, to do the "beeg t'ing". As the other boat crews watched in amazement from below, the Indians plunged over the falls, through the maelstrom, and swept out of sight around the bend of the river. Working rapidly, they reached shore and nearly emptied their boat of water. When the other crews broke through the bushes "there stood Sebattis and his bowman leaning on their paddles like bronze caryatids,

MAP
1

one on either side of the boat". This was a direct challenge to the pride of the others, and without a word they hauled their two bateaux back up to the head of the falls and tried the run as well. With two full crews of six to a boat, luck was not theirs and both boats were battered to kindling. Eleven men reached shore battered and bruised by rocks and logs, the twelfth drowned. As the story goes, the woods boss was not so upset with the loss of the men, as they were replaceable, but the loss of the boats was hard to take! Today, hundreds of people each year raft the West Branch including Nesowadnehunk Falls.

RAINBOW STREAM   The watershed of Rainbow Stream was logged extensively though the 1800s. The logging process created piles of slash (smaller branches and debris not suitable for market) which were left on the ground. The slash dried and created a serious fire hazard for all woods travelers. The outstanding open views from Rainbow Ledges and from Rainbow Mountain are the result of the Great Fire of 1923. The trail description in the 1953 edition of the *Guide to the A.T. in Maine* states that the shores of Rainbow Lake "have been burned and the resulting desolation impresses in an unforgettable fashion the need for extreme care in the woods."

Rainbow Stream, still showing dynamited ledges and steel drift pins from old log drives of the 1800s, has been memorialized in song as a difficult place to drive logs. The hardships of the men who broke the jams, ran the logs, stood waist deep in ice-cold rivers from daylight to dark, and "camped" beside the rivers in the melting snows were legendary. This lifestyle developed a distinctive type — the river driver — at his best in whitewater and where danger threatened.

DRIVING LOGS ON RAINBOW

O, April on the first day brought
From farther down a helluva lot
Of lousy, ill-begotten men
    For driving logs on Rainbow.

MAP
1

'Twas April on the second day
Old Woodman to these men did say:
'I will not give but a dollar a day
    For driving logs on Rainbow.

The men they then did curse and swear,
And in their anger they declared
They'd hang old Woodman, if they dared,
    All on the River Rainbow.

O, Rainbow that's an awful place,
And down the stream the men do race;
They couldn't get time to wash their face,
    All in the River Rainbow.

O, Rainbow that's a terrible hole,
And down the stream the logs do roll;
They always jam in the Devil's Punch Bowl
    Upon the River Rainbow.

This song was probably written in the 1870s. It was collected and published by Fannie Hardy Eckstorm & Mary Winslow Smyth, in *Minstrelsy of Maine,* published in 1927.

NAHMAKANTA LAKE Nahmakanta Lake is a good example of the speed with which access has increased throughout the Maine Woods. The current Nahmakanta Lake Camps, nearly 100 years old, occupy the site of the camp of a famous Penobscot Indian, Louis Ketchum (see "Working Nights" in *The Penobscot Man* by Fannie Hardy Eckstorm). Until the advent of float planes in the 1930s, the camps were reached from Millinocket by a long boat trip down Pemadumcook Lake, followed by a one mile carry to Third Debsconeag Lake, a half mile carry into Fourth Debsconeag Lake, and a mile and a half carry over to Nahmakanta Lake. Now, logging roads easily reach the site.

In the fall of 1990, the Land for Maine's Future Board, the Bureau of Public Lands (BPL), and the National Park Service

MAP

1

purchased nearly 30,000 acres surrounding the lake. This purchase preserves one of the most beautiful lakes along the A.T. and protects the view-shed for the Trail. The National Park Service ownership extends along the A.T. and includes the entire shoreline of the lake with the exception of the immediate area around Nahmakanta Lake Camps (privately owned and operated).

Long term management of this special use area will include the Maine Bureau of Parks and Lands (BP&L) and the National Park Service (NPS) through the MATC. A joint management plan is currently being developed for the Nahmakanta area. It is anticipated that special regulations may apply to this area from the bridge over Pollywog Stream to Nahmakanta Lake — particularly with regard to camping. Hikers should be alert for posted signs.

The history of logging in the Nahmakanta Valley coincided with that along the West Branch of the Penobscot. In 1867, the Nahmakanta Dam Company built dams on Rainbow Lake, Pollywog Pond, and Nahmakanta Lake to better control the water flow and the movement of logs to the mills. Often, a boom of logs from the upper part of the valley was towed the length of Nahmakanta Lake and released with the spring flood waters for the drive down Nahmakanta Stream, ultimately reaching Pemadumcook Lake and the West Branch of the Penobscot. Signs of the early logs drives are still visible along Nahmakanta Stream.

NESUNTABUNT MOUNTAIN The view from the ledges at the summit of Nesuntabunt is worth a rest stop. Directly below the overlook is the expanse of Nahmakanta Lake, stretching from the camps at the northwest end to the beginning of Nahmakanta Stream at the southeast end. Katahdin, clearly visible over the lake, is only 16 air miles, but 35 trail miles away as the Trail meanders through the lake country to the north. To the east, lie Pemadumcook Lake and Millinocket.

The northern slopes of Nesuntabunt Mountain feature an exemplary stand of old-growth red spruce and white pine. Some specimens are at least 140 years old, with red spruce averaging

MAP

1

17 inches and white pine 23 inches in diameter. The ten acre stand lies entirely within the A.T. corridor and has been recommended for critical area designation and protection.

References and Suggested Reading

Avery, Myron H., "Katahdin and Its History", *In the Maine Woods*, Bangor and Aroostook R.R. Co., Bangor, ME, 1939, pp. 18–26. [Ed. Note, This annual by B & A R.R. Co. is a valuable historic record of the development of the Appalachian Trail in Maine from 1928–1939.]

Caldwell, Bill, *Rivers of Fortune*, Guy Gannett Publishing, Portland, ME, 1983, 265 pages.

Clark, Stephen, *Katahdin: A Guide to Baxter Park and Katahdin*, North Country Press, Unity, ME, 1985, 313 pages.

Eckstorm, Fannie Hardy, *The Penobscot Man*, Jordan-Frost Printing Co., Bangor, ME, 1924, p. 19, 351 pages.

Eckstorm, Fannie Hardy, and Smyth, Mary Winslow, *Minstrelsy of Maine,* Houghton Mifflin, 1927, p.62, 390 pages.

Field, David B. et al, *The Natural and Cultural Resources of the Appalachian Trail Corridor in Maine,* Univ. of Maine, Orono ME, 1989 (Draft) 181 pages. [Ed. note: This extensive work, completed for the National Park Service, includes an outstanding bibliography of trail related information.]

Hakola, John W., *Legacy Of A Lifetime — The Story of Baxter State Park,* TBW Books, Woolwich, ME, 1981, 409 pages.

Pike, R.E., *Tall Trees, Tough Men*, W.W. Norton Co., New York, NY, 288 pages.

Smith, D.C., *A History of Lumbering in Maine, 1861–1960*, University of Maine Press, Orono, ME, 1972, 469 pages.

Sutton, Myron and Ann, *The Appalachian Trail*, Lippincott, New York, NY, 1967, 180 pages.

Thoreau, Henry David, *The Maine Woods*, Harper and Row, New York, NY, 1987 (paper) [reprint from Ticknor and Fields, 1864].

MAP 2
South End of Nahmakanta Lake to West Branch of the Pleasant River

Location

North central Maine, approximately 20 miles (by air) west of Millinocket.

MAP

2

Section Information

This map consists solely of Section 3.

	Section 3
Length	43.3 miles
Hiking Time	3–4 days
Elevation Gain	
Southbound	4,800 ft.
Northbound	4,800 ft.
Lean-tos & Campsites	8
Major Peaks	White Cap Range including:
White Cap Mountain	(3,654 ft.)
Hay Mountain	(3,244 ft.)
West Peak	(3,178 ft.)
Gulf Hagas Mountain	(2,683 ft.)

Trail Overview

Southbound from Nahmakanta Lake, the Trail parallels Nahmakanta Stream for nearly 5 miles, passing Nahmakanta Stream Campsite near the midpoint. After crossing the outlet of a beaver flowage near the old Mahar Tote Road, the Trail passes close to Pemadumcook Lake, one of the largest lakes along the entire A.T. The view of Katahdin across the lake is well worth the effort required by a short side trail. Beyond the crossing of Twitchell Brook and a recent logging road, another short side trail leads to the lean-to at Potaywadjo Spring. The flowing spring, 15 feet in diameter, is the largest along the Trail in Maine. From the height of land south of the lean-to, the Trail descends toward Lower Jo-Mary Lake where a short side trail leads to a fine sand beach. Near the end of the lake, a side trail leads 1 mile north to Potaywadjo Ridge, with outstanding views of the area and good blueberries in season. The Trail continues around the lake to the former site of the old Antlers Camps, now an A.T. campsite, situated on a prominent point in a majestic grove of red pine.

South of Antlers Campsite the Trail leaves the big lakes and follows the valley of Cooper Brook for 9 miles along a classic tote road dating from the 1800s. Four miles from Antlers, the Trail crosses the Jo-Mary Road, the main access road in the area. Just south of Church Pond, the route begins the easy climb from the relatively flat lake country to Cooper Brook Falls and lean-to. The lean-to is perched on a ledge overlooking the pool at the base of the cascade. The Trail continues up Cooper Brook to Crawford Pond with its glacial esker and resulting sand beaches, crosses a branch of the B Pond Road, and makes the 750 foot climb of Little Boardman Mountain. From Little Boardman, the Trail descends, passing Mountain View Pond and then descends further into the broad valley of the East Branch of the Pleasant River. South of the East Branch Lean-to, the A.T. reaches a fork of the West Branch Ponds Road and begins the three mile climb to the summit of White Cap Mountain. The route first follows Logan Brook to Logan Brook lean-to, and finally ascends the shoulder of White Cap Mountain. The open summit of White Cap affords outstanding views of Katahdin and the lake country to the north, the White Cap Range, Barren–Chairback Range and even Moxie Bald to the south. The Trail traverses the four peaks of the White Cap Range, and descends along Gulf Hagas Brook for 4 miles to the Gulf Hagas Trail. The Gulf is a spectacular slate gorge carved by the West Branch of the Pleasant River, and is one of the most outstanding natural features along the A.T. The ford of the West Branch of the Pleasant River marks the south end of Section 3.

Notable features of this Section include: Nahmakanta Lake

and Stream, Potaywadjo Spring, Lower Jo-Mary Lake, Cooper Brook Falls, esker and beaches at Crawford Pond, White Cap Mountain Range, and Gulf Hagas.

Road Access

Section 3 passes through the Katahdin Iron Works/Jo-Mary Multiple Use Management Forest. The gravel logging roads in this region are private roads open to the public by permit. For information on fees, gate hours, and current road conditions, contact North Maine Woods, P.O. Box 421, Ashland, ME, 04732.

The Jo-Mary Road is the prominent gravel road leaving Maine Highway 11 about 18 miles north of Brownville Junction or 13 miles south of Millinocket. The Jo-Mary Check Point entry gate (fee) provides access to the A.T. at three points on this map including (1) the south end of Nahmakanta Lake, the northern end of Section 3, (2) the A.T. crossing of the Jo-Mary Road at Cooper Brook, and (3) the A.T. crossing of the Kokadjo–B Pond Road at Crawford Pond. A fourth access may be possible for high clearance vehicles at the A.T. crossing of the fork of the West Branch Ponds Road near Logan Brook. From the gate, it is about 12 miles northwest to the A.T. crossing at Cooper Brook, and a further 12 miles to the south end of Nahmakanta Lake. Active logging is occurring in this forest. Check with the gatekeeper for directions and current road conditions.

To reach the north end of Section 3 at Nahmakanta Lake from Greenville, go north on the Lily Bay Road through Kokadjo. About 3 miles north of Kokadjo turn right (east) towards Second Roach Pond. Reach a four way intersection in about 5 miles. Turn left (north) and reach the intersection just west of Penobscot Pond in approximately 7 miles. Turn left (north) passing north of Penobscot Pond, reaching the Jo-Mary Road in about 3 miles. Turn left (north) toward Nahmakanta Lake. Take a right turn in about 1 mile for access to the parking area at the south end of Nahmakanta Lake, or continue straight to cross the A.T. near Nesuntabunt Mountain or to reach Pollywog Stream.

**MAP
2**

MAP

2

The ford of the West Branch of the Pleasant River, the southern end of Section 3, is reached by a 0.2 mile side trail from the West Branch trailhead parking area.

The best access to the Gulf Hagas area is through Katahdin Iron Works. From Brownville Junction, follow Maine Highway 11 north 5.5 miles, or from Millinocket, follow Maine Highway 11 south for 25.6 miles to the sign for Katahdin Iron Works. Turn west off Maine Highway 11 and follow gravel road for 6.8 miles to the entry gate at the Katahdin Iron Works historic site (KIW). Fees are collected at the gatehouse for use of the private roads and for "drive in" campsites beyond this point.

From Katahdin Iron Works proceed west across the bridge over the West Branch and turn right. At 3.0 miles take the left fork to reach the south side of the West Branch or take the right fork for the north side of the river.

South side of the river (left fork): reach the West Branch parking area at 6.7 miles from KIW. From the parking area, a blue-blazed side trail leads 0.2 miles to the A.T. ford of the West Branch of the Pleasant River.

North side of the river (right fork): cross the "High Bridge" over White Brook at 5.8 miles from KIW. Turn left (downstream) reaching the Hay Brook parking area at the end of the road 8.2 miles from KIW. A blue-blazed side trail leads 0.7 miles west meeting the A.T. near the Hermitage. This route allows access to Gulf Hagas without fording the West Branch.

Access to the north side of White Cap Mountain near Logan Brook: From Greenville proceed north on the Lily Bay Road toward the settlement of Kokadjo. At 18 miles from Greenville turn east on Frenchtown Road which parallels the south shore of First Roach Pond. At a fork at 9.3 miles bear left on the West Branch Ponds Road, and at 10.0 miles pass the driveway to West Branch Ponds Camps on the right. At 10.8 miles bear right at a fork and cross the headwaters of the West Branch of the Pleasant River between First and Second West Branch Ponds. At 12.6 miles cross Slaughter Brook and a yarding area for a recent logging operation. High clearance vehicles may be necessary beyond this point, about 2.0 miles from the A.T. Keep right at the next fork, cross Logan Brook, and park off the roadway at the vehicle barrier. Follow the road on foot about 0.5 mile east to the A.T. crossing.

Supply Points, Accommodations, and Mail Drops

MAP
2

There are no supply points between Abol Bridge (Map 1) and Monson (Map 3), a distance of over 100 miles. *Hikers in either direction should carry a supply of food sufficient to reach either destination.*

There are many "drive in" campsites (fees charged) in the Katahdin Iron Works/Jo-Mary Multiple Use Management Forest. For information contact the management agency for the area, North Maine Woods, P.O. Box 421, Ashland, Maine, 04732.

There is no mail drop near the Trail between Millinocket (north end of Map 1) and Monson (south end of Map 3).

Side Trails

Potaywadjo Ridge Trail (1.0 mile) climbs northwest to open ledges with excellent views of Jo-Mary Mountain and the surrounding lake country. Good blueberries available in season.

White Brook Trail (5.7 miles from High Bridge to the A.T.) provides access to White Cap Mountain from the valley of the West Branch of the Pleasant River. From Katahdin Iron Works proceed west across the bridge over the West Branch and turn right. At 3.0 miles take the right fork, leaving the main haul road. Cross the "High Bridge" over White Brook at 5.8 miles from Katahdin Iron Works. Trail mileage starts here. Follow the haul road upstream on the west side of White Brook by vehicle or on foot as conditions warrant. Under the best conditions, vehicles must be left well off the road at a point 3.8 miles above High Bridge where the road crosses two brooks. The trail follows the old logging road for 1.0 mile to a yarding area. Here it becomes a footpath, and in 0.4 mile, crosses White Brook near the remains of an old cabin. The trail continues to climb for 0.5 mile to the junction with the A.T. in the sag between White Cap and Hay Mountains. The summit of White Cap is 1.1 miles north on the A.T.

Gulf Hagas Cut-off Trail (1.0 mi.) Links the head of Gulf Hagas with the A.T. It provides a route for southbound hikers to reach the Head of the Gulf and for northbound hikers to return to the A.T. from the Head of the Gulf.

MAP
2

Gulf Hagas Trail (5.2 mi. round trip from the A.T.) The Gulf is a spectacular slate gorge carved by the West Branch of the Pleasant River, and is one of the most outstanding natural features along the A.T. Round trip distance from the parking area near the ford of the West Branch is 8.2 miles. This clockwise description follows the trail along the rim first, returning along the old Pleasant River tote road. (Detailed area map on Map 2.)

GULF HAGAS LOOP
Trail Description

Mileage

0.0	Trail junction with A.T. 1.3 miles north of the West Branch of the Pleasant River ford. Cross Gulf Hagas Brook to a fork in the trail. Left, the trail along the rim leads toward Screw Auger Falls and views of the Gulf, ahead is the old Pleasant River Tote Road to the Head of the Gulf.
0.1	Side trail to upper end of Screw Auger Falls on Gulf Hagas Brook. Just S, side trail leads to midpoint of the cascades.
0.2	Side trail to lower end of Screw Auger Falls.
0.7	Side trail 100 yds. to view of Hammond Street Pitch at the deepest part of the Gulf.
0.9	Junction with 150 ft. short cut to old Pleasant River tote road.
1.1	Sharp turn in trail. Side trail to view point.
1.2	Side trail to view of the Jaws.
1.4	View of the Jaws.
1.5	View of Indian Head and the Jaws.
1.8	View point of Buttermilk Falls.
1.9	View of Stair Falls.

2.2	Large pool.
2.7	View of Billings Falls.
2.8	Ledge above Billings Falls.
2.9	View Head of the Gulf.
3.0	Junction with Pleasant River tote road. Former side trail west toward Lyford Pond is closed.
3.9	Junction w/Gulf Hagas Cut-off Trail leading 1.0 mile to A.T.
4.6	Junction with 150 ft. short cut to rim trail.
5.2	Junction with rim trail. This completes the loop. Across Gulf Hagas Brook is the junction with the A.T. 1.3 miles north of the West Branch of the Pleasant River ford.

MAP

2

Points of Interest

KATAHDIN IRON WORKS/JO-MARY MULTIPLE USE MANAGEMENT FOREST In sections 3 and 4, the A.T. passes through a cooperatively managed forest which stretches from Nahmakanta Lake to Fourth Mountain on the Barren–Chairback range. The area encompasses roughly 210,000 acres owned and/or managed by at least 10 major landowners ranging from large logging companies to the National Park Service. In some areas, acreage is held in undivided ownership with shares held by paper companies and heirs to "original owners" who were granted land when Maine separated from Massachusetts in 1820.

The early 1970s marked the end of the river drives as a way to move wood to market. The resulting expansion of logging roads has dramatically increased the accessibility of this area. Most of these roads are open to the public (fees charged).

GULF HAGAS The deeply entrenched slate canyon on the West Branch of the Pleasant River is known as Gulf Hagas. The precipitous cliffs, waterfalls and interesting rock formations make it one of the most outstanding natural features along the Appalachian Trail. In 1968, the Gulf was made part of the National Natural Scenic Register, and the landowners agreed to exclude the canyon and a buffer zone from future logging operations. In 1986, the National Park Service acquired nearly 2,000 acres, including the Gulf and the corridor along Gulf Hagas Brook, to provide long term protection for its outstanding natural features.

The West Branch of the Pleasant River drops 500 feet along its three mile length before its confluence with Gulf Hagas Brook. The slate walls of the Gulf tower as high as 150 feet above the river and, just east of the Hammond Street Pitch, the valley is nearly 400 feet deep.

MAP
2

This area was first logged for its large pines in the early 1800s. The Gulf was a popular excursion point from the 1840s to the 1890s when the nearby Katahdin Iron Works was in operation. The old Pleasant River Road, now part of the Gulf Hagas Trail and the A.T., was built in 1873 to provide better access to the second cut of timber in the valley. The first logging camp at the head of the Gulf was built in 1880. Many of the falls and other features of the Gulf were named by the early loggers.

The approach to the Gulf from the A.T. starts at Gulf Hagas Brook. Immediately downstream from the crossing is a series of seven cascades alternating with shady pools. The aptly named Screw Auger Falls passes over a steep 26 foot pitch where eons of spring runoffs have carved the letter 'S' into the rock ledge. At the correct water level the lower end of the 'S' projects the water away from the wall. Below the cascade is a curious pool with square shaped walls.

The Gulf itself, located on the West Branch of the Pleasant River, extends above the confluence with Gulf Hagas Brook. The view is impressive from the precipitous Hammond Street Pitch once used as a chute to move logs into the West Branch over 100 feet below. In the past, people reported the profile of an Old Man on the higher cliff across the river. Perhaps he has changed with time.

Upstream, on the West Branch, is the narrowest spot in the canyon, called 'The Jaws'. It was originally only 7 feet 7 inches wide, and was blasted to a width of 26 feet making the passage of logs more feasible. Several short side trails lead to different views of each of the three 'Jaws'. The narrow slab above the 'Lower Jaws' forms the projecting profile of the Indian Head.

The canyon narrows above 'The Jaws', and each of the falls — Buttermilk, Stair, and Billings — provides a different view of the hydraulic forces scouring the canyon. Buttermilk Falls offers an outstanding pool at its base. Stair is a classic cascade leaping from ledge to ledge and pool to pool. The open ledges above Billings Falls offer a great viewpoint of the narrow sluice that drops its water into a huge circular bowl. At a prominent rocky island in the river, the trail reaches the Head of the Gulf. From the large pool, the trail turns away from the river to rejoin the old Pleasant River tote road for the return to the A.T.

ANTLERS CAMPSITE Antlers Campsite on Lower Jo-Mary Lake is on the site of "Potter's Antlers Camps", known for its excellent fishing. The camp was closed in 1949, but several buildings remained available for use by the public until the 1970s. Remnants of the old lodge can still be seen in the large clearing near the lake.

From the late 1800s through the early 1950s, a series of sporting camps were built throughout the Maine Wilderness. The camps catered to people of reasonably affluent means who stayed for extended periods to hunt, fish, sightsee, and relax. The camps usually consisted of a large main dining and cooking building, patrons' camps, a guides' camp and other buildings. During the early part of the 1900s, work crews built crude roads through the woods so camps could be accessed by automobile. These roads, known as corduroy roads, were made by felling cedar trees and laying them cross-wise to provide traction through boggy areas. Much of the original A.T. in Maine was routed along a series of camps taking advantage of the already cleared "corduroy roads." These byways of a bygone era can still be seen along parts of the trail from Crawford Pond to Jo-Mary Lake.

These old public hunting and fishing camps have been a part of Maine's history for over a century. Many are still in operation throughout the state, but none are located directly on the A.T. The camps at Nahmakanta Lake are the only public

MAP
2

sporting camps within the Trail corridor. The old camps, listed below from north to south, remain an important part of the history of the Appalachian Trail.

MAP
2

York's Twin Pine Camps at Daicey Pond — Now operating as a campsite with cabins in Baxter State Park; site of the 1939 Appalachian Trail Conference.

Clifford's Rainbow Lake Camps — Currently private; long-time proprietor Fred L. Clifford drowned in Rainbow Lake in the fall of 1945; the camps remained open to the public until 1948.

Clifford's Rainbow Dam Camps — Formerly Boynton's Camps, no longer exist.

Nevel's Nahmakanta Lake Camps — Formerly McDougall's Nahmakanta Camps. The only camps in the A.T. corridor still operating and open to the public, see Map 1 Points of Interest — Nahmakanta Lake.

Myshrall's White House Camps — across from Mahar Landing on Pemadumcook Lake; no longer on the Trail route.

Potter's Antlers Camps — On Lower Jo-Mary Lake, closed in 1949, but intermittently reopened until the 1970s. Most of the structures were moved to another site in the 1980s; now an A.T. campsite.

Berry's Yoke Ponds Camps — Now a private camp; closed to the public in the 1960s; no longer on the Trail route.

Chadwick's Outlying Camps — on Third West Branch Pond; no longer on the Trail route.

The Hermitage — Near Gulf Hagas was not part of the Trail's camp system.

Chairback Mountain Camps — Formerly Long Pond Camps, or Perham's Camps; privately owned; no longer on the Trail route.

Dore's Mountain View Camps — on Long Pond; no longer on the Trail route.

Troutdale Camps — At the east end of the ferry across Moxie Pond; closed in 1941; no longer on the Trail route.

Folsom's Camps — On the west side of Moxie Pond; closed

in 1945; no longer on the Trail route.

Sterling's Pierce Pond Camps — Open to the public, and operating as Harrison's Pierce Pond Camps, on the outlet stream of Pierce Pond; adjacent to the Trail corridor.

Mitchell's Pierce Pond Camps — Open to the public and operating as Cobb's Pierce Pond Camps on the western shore of Pierce Pond; no longer on the Trail route.

East Carry Camps (Steele's) — Individually-owned private camps; Trail now skirts the opposite side of the lake.

West Carry Pond Camps — Now a private camp, adjacent to the Trail corridor.

Ledge House — On the original Route 16; opened in 1895; inundated by the creation of Flagstaff Lake in 1950.

Redington Pond Camps — Closed to the public in 1950; now included in an area serving as a U.S. Navy survival training base.

COOPER BROOK LOGGING OPERATIONS The A.T. follows portions of the old Cooper Brook tote road which ran from B Pond over the Crawford Pond dam, along Cooper Brook and on to Upper Jo-Mary Lake.

The logging road was built to accommodate the Lombard log hauler, a steam locomotive developed in Waterville, Maine. The log hauler was mounted on lagged tracks and was the forerunner of World War I tanks and the crawler tractor. The machine was used extensively in the early years of this century to haul long sled trains of logs and pulpwood out of the north woods.

Old driving dams were located at the outlets of Church Pond and Cooper Pond. Between Church Pond and Cooper Brook Falls the Trail passes directly through the site of an old lumber camp abandoned after the last log drive on Cooper Brook in 1923.

ESKER AT CRAWFORD POND The high ridge at the south end of Crawford Pond is a good example of a glacial feature known as an esker. The ridge, a deposit of gravel and boulders, is the former bed of a river flowing within or under a glacier. This ridge was literally left high and dry by the retreating continental ice sheet. Since the retreat of the ice sheet, the waters of Crawford Pond have assisted in forming two sand beaches on either side of the esker. The beaches are the former stream sediments from the glacial river. Crawford Pond is a no camping zone.

MAP

2

Other prominent eskers crossed by the Trail are along Bald Mountain Stream (Map 4), between East Carry Pond and West Carry Pond (Map 5), near Bog Brook just east of Little Bigelow Mountain (Map 5), and south of Stratton Brook (Map 5).

SIDNEY TAPPAN CAMPSITE Sidney Tappan was a hard working volunteer who served as Overseer of the eastern section of the Appalachian Trail in Maine from 1952–1971. (In those years, the Trail in Maine had only two overseers for the whole state.)

In August 1963, he and Jean Stephenson, a long-time editor of the Maine guidebook, met with ATC Chairman Stanley Murray at a camp on nearby Long Pond. By lantern light, they plotted a strategy to acquire a protective corridor for the Appalachian Trail. Mr. Murray later wrote that his camping companions could foresee no other likely means to acquire a protective corridor except to "put the responsibility where the money is — with the federal government." Through the efforts of many other volunteers and politicians, the National Trails System Act was eventually passed in September, 1968.

The spring for Sidney Tappan Campsite is the headwaters for Gulf Hagas Brook. Finding it requires a steep descent down a side trail south of the campsite.

CARL A. NEWHALL LEAN-TO The Carl A. Newhall Lean-to is named for a tireless and dedicated volunteer of the MATC. A native of Peabody, Massachusetts, Carl A. Newhall, Jr. (July 27, 1919–April 24, 1985) first developed an interest in the A.T. while working in Vermont. He joined the MATC in the late 1950s.

Hundreds of hikers enjoyed his detailed, hand-written responses to their questions during his ten years as the MATC's Corresponding Secretary. Thousands have been grateful for the shelters that were built with his skillful hands: Rainbow Stream, Wadleigh Stream, Logan Brook, Pierce Pond, Hall Mountain and Frye Notch. His technique for painting blazes was legendary — leading hikers to ask if the MATC used templates!

Carl was awarded honorary membership in the Appalachian Trail Conference in July, 1981. Honorary membership in the ATC has been granted to only 40 other individuals in the 71 year history of the ATC. It is awarded only to those who have given "above and beyond the call of duty" to the Appalachian Trail or to the Conference. Fittingly, the award was presented at a beach on Nahmakanta Lake during a work trip. Carl could always be counted on to be ready when there was work to be done. He exemplified the volunteer spirit which is so crucial to the success of the Appalachian Trail project.

THE HERMITAGE Located on the north side of the West Branch of the Pleasant River, the Hermitage is a stately growth of tall white pine owned by the Maine Chapter of the Nature Conservancy.

This grove was the home of a red-haired Scot named Campbell Young, who arrived around 1890, apparently seeking solitude. His isolated cabin, overlooking the West Branch of the Pleasant River, became known as "The Hermitage", although he lived there for only a few years. In the 1920s this location was a sportsman's camp. In 1941, Mrs. Sara Green purchased the property for use by her family and friends. She transferred it to the Nature Conservancy in 1967. A bronze plaque on a large boulder commemorates the site as a National Natural Landmark. The Hermitage is a no camping zone.

KATAHDIN IRON WORKS (KIW) The development of the Iron Works began with the discovery of ore in 1843 about a mile to the west. During the first decade, growth of the accompanying settlement was rapid. The village grew to include a hotel, several stores, sawmill, blacksmith shop, and a barn with stalls for 75 horses. The thriving center of industry supported several mills and foundries, and the iron works included the massive blast furnace and eight two story high charcoal kilns.

With the competition located closer to population centers, the success of the iron works was short lived. Several major fires

MAP
2

interrupted production in 1856. In the early 1860s, the discovery of a new method for producing high quality steel from low grade ore spelled doom for the entire New England iron industry. Lower grade ores in Minnesota and Pennsylvania provided more economical sources of iron.

MAP
2

Today the only remains on this once thriving site are the roasting blast furnace and a huge beehive charcoal kiln. The state of Maine has erected a memorial to mark the Katahdin Iron Works State Historical Site. The keeper at the nearby gate house, operated by North Maine Woods, provides information and permits for the Katahdin Iron Works/Jo-Mary Multiple Use Management Forest to the west.

References and Suggested Reading

Cummings, R.C., "Gulf Hagas: Maine's Hidden Wonder", *Maine Sunday Telegram*, Portland, ME, October, 13, 1986.

Cummings, R.C., "Scenic Canyon Pegged To Become Mini National Park", *Maine Sunday Telegram*, Portland, ME, January 19, 1986, p.16A.

Hubbard, L.L., *Guide To Moosehead Lake And Northern Maine Wilderness*, 4th Ed., A. Williams & Co., 1882, pp. 151–155, 206 pp.

King, Brian B., "1968 Legislation Set Stage for National System of Trails", *Appalachian Trailway News*, Appalachian Trail Conference, Harpers Ferry, WV, May/June 1993, p. 18.

Lebourdias, Richard, "A Ghost Town in Maine", *Maine Sunday Telegram*, Portland, ME, October, 17, 1948.

Robinson, William F., *Abandoned New England: Its Hidden Ruins and Where to Find Them*, New York Graphic Society, Boston, MA, 1976, 211 pages.

Sawtell, William R., *Katahdin Iron Works Revisited*, Milo Printing Co., Milo, ME, 1983, 148 pages.

Worthington, W.J., "Katahdin Iron Works", *Appalachia*, vol. 22, no. 3, 1939, Appalachian Mountain Club, Boston, MA. [Ed. note: This is a detailed illustrated account of the development of Katahdin Iron Works.]

MAP 3
West Branch of the Pleasant River to Monson

Location
North central Maine, just northeast of Monson.

Section Information
This map consists solely of Section 4.

MAP

3

	Section 4
Length	30.4 miles
Hiking Time	2–3 days
Elevation Gain	
Southbound	5,900 ft.
Northbound	5,100 ft.
Lean-tos & Campsites	5
Major Peaks	Barren–Chairback Range including:
	Chairback Mountain (2,219 ft.)
	Columbus Mountain (2,326 ft.)
	Third Mountain (2,061 ft.)
	Fourth Mountain (2,383 ft.)
	Barren Mountain (2,670 ft.)

Trail Overview
From the ford of the West Branch of the Pleasant River, the Trail turns upstream and parallels the river before crossing the haul road from Katahdin Iron Works. To the south, the Trail ascends out of the valley of the West Branch of the Pleasant River and begins the traverse of the 15 mile long Barren–Chairback Range. Although the five major peaks are all under 3,000 ft. in elevation, this section of Trail involves significant gain and loss of elevation over a rough footway. Despite the relatively low elevation of the range, it includes an interesting variety of mountain terrain, tarns, bogs, hardwood forests, softwood forests, ledges, cliffs, and frequent views. From Barren

MAP

3

Mountain at the south end of the range, the Trail descends to Long Pond Stream and Bodfish Valley.

The southern 15 miles of this section traverses a series of low slate ridges and deep valleys. Several large streams, such as Long Pond Stream and Big Wilson Stream, can be difficult or dangerous to cross in high water. Spectacular waterfalls have been formed by the streams in the slate valleys. After traversing a series of slate ridges, the Trail then passes a number of small ponds before crossing Maine Highway 15 between Monson and Greenville. South of Highway 15, the Trail climbs a shoulder of Doughty Hill and then Buck Hill before reaching Lake Hebron west of Monson. Most thru-hikers choose to make a side trip into Monson as it is the most convenient place to re-supply between Millinocket and Caratunk.

Notable features of this Section include: the Barren–Chairback range and the interesting natural features formed by the slate ridges north of Monson including spectacular Little Wilson Falls.

Road Access

The ford of the West Branch of the Pleasant River, the northern end of Section 4, is reached by a 0.2 mile side trail from the Gulf Hagas trailhead parking area.

The best access to the Gulf Hagas area is through Katahdin Iron Works. From Brownville Junction, follow Maine Highway 11 north 5.5 miles, or from Millinocket, follow Maine Highway 11 south for 25.6 miles to the sign for Katahdin Iron Works. Turn west off Maine Highway 11 and follow the gravel road for 6.8 miles to the entry gate at the Katahdin Iron Works historic site. A fee is collected at the gatehouse for use of the private roads and campsites beyond this point.

From Katahdin Iron Works proceed west across the bridge over the West Branch and turn right. At 3.0 miles take the left fork and reach the Gulf Hagas and A.T. parking area at 6.7 miles. From the parking area, a blue-blazed side trail leads 0.2 mile to the A.T. ford of the West Branch of the Pleasant River.

Access at Long Pond Stream: The Elliotsville Road leaves Maine

Highway 15 about half a mile north of the center of Monson and provides access to the A.T. at Long Pond Stream. After the Elliotsville Road crosses Big Wilson Stream, a left fork bears north around Boarstone Mountain, and reaches the Bodfish Farm Site 11.8 miles from Monson. Follow the Long Pond Stream Tote Road (sometimes passable by high clearance vehicles) along Long Pond Stream, 1.6 miles northeast to the A.T.

Maine Highway 15 crosses the A.T. at the southern end of Section 4 about 3.5 miles north of Monson or about 11 miles south of Greenville. Trailhead parking is located on the east side of the highway.

MAP

3

Supply Points, Accommodations, and Mail Drops

Monson, population 500, is a key resupply point for both southbound and northbound hikers. Monson offers a general store, hardware store, laundromat, and a few restaurants.

In Monson, Shaw's Boarding Home, on Pleasant Street, caters to hikers and offers a shuttle service and "hikers supplies". See Shaw's Boarding Home, page 118, for more information.

There are no supply points north of Monson until Abol Bridge (Map 1) is reached roughly 100 miles to the north. *Northbound hikers should carry an 8–10 day supply of food. This is the longest remote section along the entire A.T.*

Greenville, a major gateway for much of the northern Maine woods, is 14 miles north of Monson on Maine Highway 15. Guilford, 14 miles southeast on Route 16, and Dover-Foxcroft, 22 miles southeast on Route 16, offer a wide range of services including supermarkets, laundromats, hardware stores and banks.

The Post Office ZIP code for Monson is 04464.

Side Trails

East Chairback Pond (0.2 mi.) Descend 200 feet to the shore of this mountain tarn, with excellent views of Chairback and Columbus mountains.

West Chairback Pond (0.2 mi.) Follow an old logging road to the shore of West Chairback Pond, a popular destination for fishermen.

Points of Interest

TARNS OF THE BARREN–CHAIRBACK RANGE Tarns are pocket-like bodies of water formed by the scouring action of a glacier. East Chairback Pond, West Chairback Pond, and Cloud Pond each has its own unique character and is well worth a visit.

MAP
3

MONUMENT CLIFF ON THIRD MOUNTAIN The memorial plaque commemorates Walter D. Greene, Broadway actor, Maine Guide, and a former President of the Maine Appalachian Trail Club. In 1933, he almost single-handedly scouted and marked the route over the Barren–Chairback Range. This accomplishment was characterized by Myron Avery as one of the great feats in the annals of trail building.

Much of the A.T. along this range fell into disuse during World War II, and with a lack of maintenance the Trail quickly filled in with new growth. Furthermore, extensive logging in the area obliterated large sections of the Trail. When the war was over and hikers returned to the woods, the Trail was temporarily relocated on logging roads along Long Pond Stream and Wilder Brook to reach the east end of the range. With much effort, the Trail was restored to its original route along the crest of Barren Mountain in 1956.

FOURTH MOUNTAIN BOG This bog located on both sides of the A.T. has some fine examples of insectivorous plants. The Pitcher Plant has specialized leaves formed in the shape of a pitcher. The curious leaves, usually 4″ to 8″ long, have hundreds of hairs which point downward, helping to trap insects in the water that collects in the pitcher shaped leaves. The pitcher plant secretes enzymes into the water assisting with the "digestion" of the insects. Another adaptation allowing the pitcher plant to thrive in the nutrient-poor bog is its association with nitrogen-fixing bacteria which allows atmospheric nitrogen to become available to the plant.

The Sundew, with small leaves at the base of the plant, is covered with reddish hairs. The hairs exude a sticky liquid that entraps insects providing the plant with added nourishment. Both of these plants are protected. Observe, but do not disturb.

BARREN MOUNTAIN FIRE TOWER   This fire warden's tower was built in 1950 to provide a lookout for wild fires following the heavy logging of this area. This region was first logged in the mid 1800s, and a second cut began in 1939 between East Chairback Pond and Long Pond. This effort was curtailed due a shortage of manpower during World War II. Following the war, nearly all of the north side of the Barren–Chairback Range from the West Chairback Pond area to Bodfish Intervale was cut for pulpwood.

MAP 3

The original A.T. in Maine passed by seven forest fire lookout towers. Many hikers enjoyed a brief respite from the elements, and from solitude, through visits with the men who spent years of their lives keeping watch from these lonely outposts for the wildfires that regularly threaten Maine's forests. None of these towers are now manned, and only two of the structures still stand. Most of the State's fire detection is now carried out from aircraft. Other summits which supported towers include White Cap, Moxie Bald Mountain, Pleasant Pond Mountain, Bigelow Mountain, Mt. Abraham, Saddleback, and Old Speck.

Maine's fire towers were built in response to devastating forest fires that swept the northeastern United States during the early 1900s. The fire tower on Squaw Mountain, visible north of the A.T. from Moxie Bald and Pleasant Pond mountains, was built in 1905, the first fire tower built in the United States. Both logging and forest fires have shaped the character of the forests along much of the A.T. in Maine.

BARREN LEDGES/BODFISH INTERVALE   Views from Barren Ledges are most striking. Bodfish Intervale stretches out below to the shores of Lake Onawa, and Boarstone Mountain rises precipitously from the south side of the Intervale. At the outlet of Lake Onawa, is the Onawa Viaduct, the highest railroad trestle east of the Rockies.

The valley was first settled in 1823 by Samuel G. Bodfish who cleared the land and built the first road into the valley. The Intervale is the former bed of a once larger Lake Onawa which geologists believe may have drained into the valley of Big Wilson Stream. The shoreline benches left by the old lake level can be discerned at roughly 700 feet above sea level.

The views of Barren Mountain are equally striking from the old Bodfish Farm site located at the junction of the Long Pond Tote Road and a branch of the Elliotsville Road.

MAP 3

CANADIAN PACIFIC RAILROAD ABOVE BIG WILSON STREAM This is the only active rail line intersecting the Trail in Maine. Maine, as elsewhere in the country, had its railroad heyday for about a century from 1830 to 1930. Both narrow gauge and standard gauge lines spread rail networks from the coast up the river valleys and into the forests of Maine. Rail lines in the interior of Maine were closely associated with the wood and lumber industry.

The Trail crosses or follows the bed of four abandoned lines:

Bangor and Aroostook line (standard gauge) from Blanchard to Greenville. This line was originally created as the Bangor and Piscataquis Railroad around 1884. The Trail crosses the railbed just above the East Branch of the Piscataquis River near Blanchard. Other branches of the Bangor and Aroostook line ran through Bangor to the northern tip of Maine.

Maine Central Railroad line (standard gauge) was a consolidation of some 50 lines which extended all over the central part of the State. One branch ran from Bingham to Moosehead Lake near Rockwood and carried a significant number of passengers. Maine Central was in both the rail business and the "destination resort" business, including the famous Kineo House on Moosehead Lake. This line was completed in 1911 and used until the rails were removed in the mid-1930s. The Trail uses this old railbed near Moxie Pond. Stations were located at Troutdale and Baker Siding.

Sandy River and Rangeley Lakes Railroad (narrow gauge)

was a consolidation of the Sandy River, Franklin & Megantic, and Phillips & Rangeley railroad lines. Areas served included: Farmington, Redington, Rangeley Village, and the Carrabassett Valley. From the 1890s to the 1930s, trains carried pulpwood, logs, freight, mail, and passengers. Improving roads and Depression losses forced the railroad out of existence in the 1930s. When the original route of the A.T. was being laid out in 1934 and 1935 across the Redington Valley, the last of the steel rails were being removed. The Trail crosses the railroad bed near Sluice Brook Falls at the end of a steady grade from Phillips, where trains climbed 1,000 feet in 2.5 miles on their way to Rangeley.

MAP

3

Rumford Falls and Rangeley Lakes Railroad (standard gauge), later part of the Maine Central Railroad, was formed to expedite removal of timber from the forests north of Rumford. The line ran up the Bemis Stream valley between Mooselookmeguntic Lake and Rangeley Lake, to Kennebago Lake. It was abandoned north of Rumford after the disastrous floods of March, 1936, and the track was removed in 1937. The Trail crosses this line approximately 1 mile west of Maine Highway 17 in the Bemis valley.

THE SLATE RIDGES FROM MONSON TO THE BARREN–CHAIRBACK RANGE The bedrock in much of the area from the West Branch of the Piscataquis River to Chairback Mountain is composed of Silurian slate. This exceptionally fine grained slate, known along the east coast as Monson Slate, is formed from sediments made more durable by the cooling of the adjacent granitic rocks. Slate mining began here in 1870 and reached its peak in the Monson area around the turn of the century. Many quarries remain in the area as testament to the large volume of slate removed for use in the building trade. The unusually black Monson Slate was used as the memorial marker for the John F. Kennedy grave site in Arlington National Cemetery.

LITTLE WILSON FALLS The highest waterfall on the A.T. and one of the highest in Maine. It is situated in a 100 foot deep slate canyon about 300 yards long with unusual rock formations and deep pools.

References and Suggested Reading

Crittenden, H. Temple, *The Maine Scenic Route*, McLain Printing Co., Parsons, WV, 1966, 229 pages. [Ed. Note: a history of the narrow gauge Sandy River and Rangeley Lakes Railroad.]

Moody, Linwood W., *The Maine Two Footers*, Howell North, Berkeley, CA, 1959, 213 pages.

Marchand, Peter, *North Woods*, Appalachian Mountain Club, Boston, MA, 1987, 141 pages, paper. [Ed. note: A guide to the nature of forests in the Northeast.]

MAP
3

MAP 4
Monson to the Kennebec River

Location
North central Maine, just west of Monson.

Section Information
This map consists solely of Section 5.

Section 5

Length	37.0 miles
Hiking Time	3 days
Elevation Gain	
Southbound	4,200 ft.
Northbound	4,500 ft.
Lean-tos & Campsites	5
Major Peaks	Moxie Bald Mountain (2,629 ft.)
	Pleasant Pond Mountain (2,477 ft.)

MAP
4

Trail Overview

Section 5 traverses wild terrain between Maine Highway 15 north of Monson and U.S. Route 201 at Caratunk near the Kennebec River. After slabbing the side of Doughty and Buck Hills and skirting to the west of Monson alongside Lake Hebron, the Trail crosses the Shirley–Blanchard road and begins the long river walk up the Piscataquis River. This route requires a ford of the East Branch of the Piscataquis just after the Shirley–Blanchard Road and a ford at the confluence of the West Branch of the Piscataquis and Bald Mountain Stream 5.4 miles later. Both of these fords require particular care in high water. The valley and stream walk along the West Branch of the Piscataquis with its deep slate canyons, falls, and quiet pools, offers good swimming and fishing. There are several large stands of "old-growth" white pine and spruce along the West Branch, east of Horseshoe Canyon lean-to. Leaving the valley of the West Branch, the A.T. parallels Bald Mountain Stream, passes Bald Mountain Pond, and traverses Moxie Bald Mountain (2,629 ft.). The long ridge of Moxie Bald offers many points of interest, including blueberries and raspberries in season. On a clear day, sweeping views are possible, from the coastal lowlands to the south, to the Barren–Chairback range, White Cap Mountain, Katahdin, Big Squaw Mountain, and the Boundary Range to the north, and to the Bigelow Range and Sugarloaf Mountain to the west. The Trail descends to Moxie Pond before traversing Pleasant Pond Mountain (2,477 ft.—views similar to Moxie Bald) and passes Pleasant Pond with good swimming opportunities nearby. Both peaks are popular as day hikes. Section 5 ends near Caratunk on the east shore of the Kennebec River.

MAP

4

Notable features of the section include the West Branch of the Piscataquis River, Moxie Bald Mountain, and Pleasant Pond Mountain.

Road Access

Maine Highway 15 crosses the A.T. at the northern end of Section 5 about 3.5 miles north of Monson or 11 miles south of Greenville. Trailhead parking is located on the east side of the highway.

Access to the West Branch of the Piscataquis: The Shirley–Blanchard Road crosses the A.T. at a point 1.3 miles north of Blanchard (crossroads). Park on the west side of the road, 0.1 mile south of the A.T. crossing.

Access at Moxie Pond: From the south, follow Route 16 northeast from U.S. Route 201 in Bingham. At 0.8 miles turn north on the Scott Paper Co. gravel road at the junction with Cassidy Road. The Scott Paper Co. road (the old Maine Central Railroad bed) crosses the A.T. 15.9 miles from Bingham. From the north, follow U.S. Route 201 to The Forks, turn east 5.3 miles to the village of Lake Moxie and turn south following the gravel road (old Maine Central Railroad bed) 7.6 miles along the west side of Moxie Pond to the A.T. crossing. The

A.T. follows the road on the southwest side of Moxie Pond for 0.2 miles. Hiker parking is just south of the A.T. on the west side of the road.

Access at Pleasant Pond: From Caratunk town center just off U.S. Route 201, follow Pleasant Pond Road (opposite the general store) 3.2 miles to the Pond and stay left at the fork. The paved road soon turns into a gravel logging road. Pass several access roads to the Pond. At a fork at 4.6 miles continue straight ahead to a hiker parking area near the north end of Pleasant Pond.

U.S. Route 201 crosses the A.T. near the south end of Section 5 at the north end of the village of Caratunk, about 16 miles north of Bingham or 7.3 miles south of The Forks. Hiker parking is located up a steep incline on the east side of the road, just north of the junction of U.S. Route 201 and old U.S. 201. The Kennebec River is the division between Sections 5 and 6.

MAP

4

Crossing the Kennebec River

The Kennebec River is the most formidable unbridged crossing along the entire 2,100 mile A.T. The Kennebec is approximately 70 yards wide with a swift, powerful current under the best of circumstances. However, as a result of releases of water from the hydro facilities upstream, the depth and current of the river surge quickly and unpredictably. You cannot cross faster than the water level rises. ***Do not attempt to ford the river.***

Returning to the historic means of crossing the river, the MATC and the Appalachian Trail Conference jointly provide a free ferry service from late May to early October. Dates and times of operation are posted annually along the Trail at nearby lean-tos and at the crossing. Further information may be obtained by writing to: MATC, P.O. Box 283, Augusta, ME 04332-0283.

Supply Points, Accommodations, and Mail Drops

Monson, population 500, is a key resupply point for both southbound and northbound hikers. Monson, at the northern end of Map 4, offers a general store, hardware store, laundro-mat, and restaurants. Shaw's Boarding Home, on Pleasant Street, caters to hikers and offers a shuttle service and "hikers' supplies". See Points of Interest below for more information.

Greenville, a major gateway for much of the northern Maine woods, is 14 miles north of Monson on Maine Highway 15. Guilford, 14 miles southeast on Route 16, and Dover-Foxcroft, 22 miles southeast on Route 16, offer a wide range of services and accommodations.

Caratunk, population 100, marks the southern end of Map 4. It is a small town with a general store and hostel. A Post Office is located in the store and may offer only part time hours of operation.

The Forks, population 30, about 7.5 miles north of Caratunk on U.S. Route 201, has small convenience stores and overnight facilities. There are cabins, a bed and breakfast, and several rafting outfitters located between Caratunk and The Forks.

Bingham, 16 miles south of Caratunk on U.S. Route 201, is a larger town with grocery, clothing, and hardware stores, a laun-dromat, restaurants, and banks.

Post Office ZIP codes: Monson, 04464; Caratunk, 04925.

MAP
4

Side Trails

North Peak Trail on Moxie Bald Mountain (0.7 mi.) leaves the A.T. 0.7 mile north of the northern junction of the Summit By-Pass Trail or 1.1 miles south of Moxie Bald Lean-to. This trail offers a pleasant ledge walk with good views, and good blueberries in season.

Summit By-Pass Trail on Moxie Bald Mountain (0.5 mi.) is an inclement weather alternative, avoiding the open summit ledges traversed by the A.T. This also offers a good loop for those day hiking on the peak.

Points of Interest

SHAW'S BOARDING HOME IN MONSON Shaw's, a leg-endary resupply point along the A.T., has hosted thousands of hikers since opening in 1978. With home-cooked meals, a washer/dryer, bunkroom or private accommodations, shuttle service, and hikers supplies, Shaw's provides welcome services to travelers either beginning or ending the 100 mile stretch between Monson and Abol Bridge. Food drop boxes may be sent directly to the Shaw's at: Pleasant Street or P.O. Box 157, Monson, ME 04464. Phone: (207) 997-3597.

BANGOR AND AROOSTOOK RAILROAD See Canadian Pacific Railroad, page 112, for more information about the history of railroads in Maine.

WEST BRANCH OF THE PISCATAQUIS RIVER The A.T. follows the bank of the West Branch of the Piscataquis River for 5 miles along one of the finest river walks in the State. Horseshoe Canyon, with slate walls up to 40 feet high, extends about 0.2 mile in both directions from the lean-to located on the largest of the four meanders of the river. At the east end, the Trail passes through a stand of large white pine. Iron pins and cables provide evidence of the early logging here. The many pools and falls offer swimming along the West Branch. (Watch for poison ivy!)

MAP 4

NATIVE AMERICAN NAMES ALONG THE TRAIL Many of the names along the A.T. originated with the Native Americans who lived and hunted in these forests. The Abenaki tribes lived throughout the land that is now New Brunswick and Maine. They were not people who left monuments to themselves for they lived simply, leaving few imprints of their passing. The colorful, but sometimes hard to pronounce names are the legacy of a people who lived in harmony with the natural world. Below are some of the place-names encountered along the Trail:

Abol — short for Aboljackarnegassic, "bare, devoid of trees"

Androscoggin — "a place where fish are cured" i.e. full of fish (salmon, shad, alewives)

Caratunk — "forbidding or crooked stream"

Carrabassett — "small moose place"

Debsconeag — "ponds at the high place"

Jo-Mary — Abenaki Chief renowned for his hunting and
  swimming abilities

Katahdin — "greatest mountain"

Kennebec — "long level water without rapids"

Kokadjo — "kettle mountains"

Mahoosuc — possibly "home of the hungry animals"

Millinocket — "dotted with many mountains" or "lake with
  many irregularities, i.e. points, coves, ledges, islands"

Mooselookmeguntic — "portage to moose feeding place"

Moxie — "dark water"

Nahmakanta — "plenty of fish" or "lake of the largest fish"

Nesowadnehunk — "swift stream between mountains"

Nesuntabunt — "three heads" (three summits)

Oquossoc — "slender blue trout"

Onawa — "awaken" in Chippewa

Pemadumcook — "extended sandbar place"

Penobscot — "descending ledge place" or "the rocky river",
  (also, name of major Native American group in this area)

Piscataquis — "at the river branch"

Potaywadjo — "wind blows over mountain" or "whale
  mountain"

Ripogenus — "small rocks, gravel"

MAP
4

PLEASANT POND MOUNTAIN, MOXIE BALD MOUNTAIN

If you ever wonder why much of the Appalachian Trail in Maine
is wet, muddy or rocky, just imagine the weight and abrasive
action of 4,000 feet of ice grinding over the landscape. The
thin soils we have today are the result of crushed rock and debris left behind as the ice sheet melted. From the summit of
Pleasant Pond Mountain or Moxie Bald Mountain, look out and
imagine a sea of glacial ice as far as the eye can see. In geologic
terms, it was just yesterday that the Native Americans followed
the retreating ice northward a mere 10,000 years ago.

The summit areas above treeline on Pleasant Pond Mountain
and Moxie Bald Mountain provide excellent exposures to both
the bedrock and glacial geology of west-central Maine.

Pleasant Pond Mountain is composed of the early Devonian Carrabassett Formation, a rock that originally formed from turbidity flows in which silts and clays were rhythmically laid down in the ocean 400 million years ago. During the Acadian Orogeny, the collision between North America and Eurasia 380 million years ago, the Appalachian Mountains were built by the heating and folding of rock such as the Carrabassett Formation. Mudstone was metamorphosed to slate, the result being the Monson slate quarries — where rock that originally lay horizontal, became vertical.

On the open ledges of Pleasant Pond Mountain, the slate was smoothed and striated by the Laurentide Ice Sheet, the last ice sheet that covered North America. The rock was beautifully molded into smooth, round knobs by the sandpapering abrasive action of rock and debris underneath the glacier. This latest glaciation lasted from approximately 25,000 to 14,000 years ago. If you orient yourself from northwest to southeast and look down at the rock, you will see grooves and striations carved into the rock — evidence that Pleasant Pond Mountain was completely covered by moving ice several thousand feet thick.

MAP
4

Moxie Bald Mountain is composed of course-grained gabbro. The major minerals are white feldspars, vitreous quartz, flaky biotite mica, and black stubby hornblende. This rock was formed by partial melting of the Eurasian plate as it was subducted under the North American plate. Magma rose and cooled slowly over several million years, allowing the large crystals to grow. Subsequent erosion of the landscape brought these rocks to the surface where we observe them today.

On the open ledges of the summit, you can see the characteristic *roche moutonnée* (literally — rock sheep) forms of the bedrock. These forms display a gentle upslope of several meters on their northwest side, and a shorter, abrupt face on their southeast side. These distinctive forms resulted from the ice sheet flowing over Moxie Bald Mountain from its central dome, 12,000 feet high above Hudson's Bay. At its maximum extent, the Laurentide Ice Sheet extended out to Georges and Browns

Banks on the offshore continental shelf, completely burying the state of Maine. Pressure melting on the upstream, or northwest side, caused the rock debris and water mixture to act as a liquid sandpaper, polishing the rough surfaces into smooth, striated slopes. As this mixture passed over the mountain's summit, pressure was relieved and refreezing occurred, plucking pieces of gabbro from the southwest side. This process is analogous to the pressure from an ice skate that causes melting under the blade and produces the skater's glide. As soon as the pressure is relieved, the thin film of water refreezes. The size of the *roche moutonnée* was determined by the regular spacing of jointing sets in the gabbro.

MAP
4

As you hike from Pleasant Pond Mountain to Moxie Bald Mountain, you pass over the contact zone where the liquid magma rose like a hot air balloon into the Carrabassett Formation. This sharp contact is in the vicinity of Bald Mountain Brook on the west side of Moxie Bald Mountain. On the east side, the contact can be seen clearly just upstream from where the Trail crosses the outlet of Bald Mountain Pond. Put your finger on the razor sharp contact and feel the abyss of time.

References and Suggested Reading

Eckstorm, Fanny Hardy, *Indian Place Names of the Penobscot Valley and the Maine Coast*, University of Maine Studies, Second Series, No. 55, 1941, reprinted 1978, 272 pages.

Eckstorm, Fanny Hardy, "Indian Names of Two Maine Mountains", *The New England Quarterly*, March, 1936.

Hubbard, Lucius L., *Woods and Lakes of Maine*, New Hampshire Publishing Co., Somersworth, NH, 1971, 223 pages (originally published by Ticknor & Co., Boston, MA, 1883).

Maine Writers Research Club, *Maine Indians in History and Legend*, Severn Wylie Jewett, Co., Portland, ME, 1942, 180 pages.

Rutherford, Philip R., *Dictionary of Maine Place Names*, Bond Wheelright Co., Freeport, ME, 1970, 283 pages.

MAP 5
Kennebec River to Maine Highway 27

Location
North central Maine, approximately 30 miles NE of Rangeley.

Section Information
Section 6: Kennebec River to Long Falls Dam Road
Section 7: Long Falls Dam Road to Maine Highway 27

	Section 6	Section 7	Map Total
Length	17.2 mi.	19.1 mi.	36.3 mi.
Hiking Time	1–2 days	2 days	3–4 days
Elevation Gain			
Southbound	2,400 ft.	6,000 ft.	8,400 ft.
Northbound	1,700 ft.	6,000 ft.	7,700 ft.
Lean-tos & Campsites	2	6	8
Major Peaks	none	Bigelow Range including:	
		Little Bigelow	(3,040 ft.)
		Avery Peak	(4,088 ft.)
		West Peak	(4,145 ft.)
		South Horn	(3,805 ft.)

MAP
5

Trail Overview

The northern terminus of Section 6 is the west side of the Kennebec River, lowest elevation along the A.T. in Maine. Ferry service across the Kennebec is available through a cooperative effort of the MATC and the Appalachian Trail Conference. Dates and times of operation are posted annually along the Trail at nearby lean-tos and at the crossing, or are available by writing the MATC. ***Fording the Kennebec is extremely hazardous. Do not attempt to ford the river.*** Because of the "flash flood" danger resulting from hydropower generation upstream, you cannot cross faster than the river rises.

From the Kennebec, the Trail parallels Pierce Pond Stream for several miles with short side trails to interesting falls and pools. South of the lean-to at Pierce Pond is the heart of the Carry Ponds area where the A.T. follows part of the Arnold Trail (commemorating Benedict Arnold's desperate march to Quebec in 1775). After a traverse of the north slope of low Roundtop Mtn. (2,240 ft.), the Trail reaches the paved Long Falls Dam Road near the southeast end of Flagstaff Lake. Availability of water in Section 6 is not a problem as numerous brook crossings are required. In fact, after a heavy rain the Trail can be very wet and muddy.

Section 7 traverses the Bigelow Range, a long east-west range consisting of six major peaks and a number of lesser ones. From east to west the peaks on the range include:

Little Bigelow Mtn.	elev. 3,040 ft.
Avery (East) Peak	elev. 4,088 ft.
West Peak	elev. 4,145 ft.
South Horn	elev. 3,805 ft.
North Horn (side trail)	elev. 3,792 ft.
Cranberry Peak (side trail)	elev. 3,213 ft.

A traverse of the range is a classic ridge walk involving substantial gain and loss of elevation.

The views from the Bigelow Range rival those from Katahdin and White Cap. There is an extensive above treeline alpine area on Avery (East) Peak and a smaller one around the West Peak. Plants are similar to those found on Katahdin and on Mt. Washington. Horns Pond, a true mountain tarn pocketed between precipitous cliffs, is nestled just west of the Horns. Cranberry Pond, located west of the A.T., is also a tarn. Most of the Range is part of the Bigelow Preserve managed by the State of Maine for multiple uses. This is a heavy use area with an active seasonal caretaker program at Horns Pond and at Bigelow Col.

Notable features of these sections include: the Kennebec River, the historic Carry Ponds area, and the Bigelow Preserve.

Road Access

U.S. Route 201 crosses the A.T. near the north end of Section 6 at the north end of the village of Caratunk, about 16 miles north of Bingham or 7.3 miles south of The Forks. Hiker parking is located up a steep incline on the east side of the road, just north of the junction of U.S. Route 201 and old U.S. 201. The Kennebec River is the division between Sections 5 and 6.

Access to Pierce Pond Stream or East Carry Pond via Bingham: A system of logging roads connects U.S. Route 201 at Bingham with the Flagstaff Lake area and Long Falls Dam Road. From Bingham, (0.0 miles), cross to the west side of the Kennebec River on Route 16, turning north along the west side of the Kennebec River. Branch right (north) at the intersection for Rowe Pond and Carry Ponds Road, 4.5 miles from Bingham. The road soon turns to gravel, and at 12.1 miles the town road ends and continues as a private logging road. The road forks again at 15.4 miles. The right fork (north) heads uphill toward Pierce Pond and crosses the A.T. at 19.4 miles from Bingham, immediately after crossing Pierce Pond Stream. The left fork (west) continues on the private logging road, crossing the A.T. at 18.2 miles from Bingham. From this crossing it is 1.7 miles south on the A.T. to the north end of East Carry Pond.

Access to Pierce Pond Stream or East Carry Pond from Long Falls Dam Road: From the junction of the Long Falls Dam Road and the gated access road to the dam facility (0.0 miles), continue north to a prominent "Y" in the road at 0.4 miles. Bear right (east) onto private gravel road. The road crosses the A.T. at 7.0 miles from the dam facility access road. From this crossing it is 1.7 miles south on the A.T. to the north end of East Carry Pond. The road continues toward the Pierce Pond area and eventually on to Bingham. Remember, there are many logging roads "not on the map," and logging trucks have the right-of-way! Never park in a way that blocks access to a road or to the roadway.

Long Falls Dam Road, the division between Sections 6 and 7, crosses the A.T. near the east end of Flagstaff Lake, 19.8

MAP

5

miles north of the village of North New Portland.

Access to north and east side of Bigelow: At 17.4 miles north of North New Portland leave the paved Long Falls Dam Road turning northwest on the gravel Bog Brook Road. At 0.7 mile the Bog Brook Road forks. The right fork crosses the A.T. 0.1 mile north, and ends a short distance beyond at an access to Flagstaff Lake. The left fork is the more heavily traveled East Flagstaff Road which intersects the A.T. in 0.1 mile. Park in a gravel pit on the east side of the road. For access to the north side of the Bigelow Range, continue west on East Flagstaff Road about 4.5 miles to the Safford Brook Trailhead just beyond the crossing of Safford Brook. The right turn just after the trailhead leads to the Round Barn public use area on the shore of Flagstaff Lake.

Access to the south side of Bigelow: Stratton Brook Pond Road is a rough gravel road which leaves Maine Highway 27 at 4.6 miles south of the junction of Highways 16 and 27 in Stratton or 0.6 mile north of the A.T. crossing of Maine Highway 27. At 1.4 miles from the highway, the Stratton Brook Pond Road crosses the A.T. At 2.1 miles reach trailhead parking for the Fire Warden's and Horns Pond Trails.

MAP
5

Maine Highway 27 crosses the A.T. at the southern end of Section 7, 5.2 miles south of the junction of Highways 16 and 27 in the village of Stratton or 18 miles north of the junction of Highways 16 and 27 in the town of Kingfield. Park on the old road on the west side of Highway 27.

Supply Points, Accommodations, and Mail Drops

Caratunk, population 100, marks the northern end of Map 5. It is a small town with a general store and hostel. A Post Office with limited hours is located in the store. Cabins, a bed and breakfast, and a rafting outfitter are located about 3 miles to the north.

The Forks, about 8 miles north of Caratunk, has small convenience stores.

Bingham, 16 miles south of Caratunk on U.S. Route 201, is a larger town with grocery, clothing, and hardware stores, a laundromat, restaurants, and banks.

North New Portland, a small village 19.8 miles south of the A.T. crossing of Long Falls Dam Road includes campgrounds, inns, and convenience stores.

Stratton, population 700, is 5 miles north of the A.T. on Maine Highway 27. Stratton has restaurants, inns and motels, two grocery stores and a laundromat. There is a campground on the shore of Flagstaff Lake about 5 miles north of the village near Eustis.

Post Office ZIP codes: Caratunk, 04925; Stratton, 04982.

Side Trails

Safford Brook Trail (2.5 mi.) This trail on the north side of the Bigelow range partially follows the old "Dead River Route," part of the A.T. in the 1930s. The trail climbs gradually, crossing Safford Brook 0.7 mile above East Flagstaff road, and then more steeply to the junction with the A.T. in Safford Notch. Southbound from the junction it is 1.1 miles to the Old Man's Head and an additional 0.8 mile to Avery Peak. Northbound from the junction, Safford Notch Campsite is 0.3 mile.

Fire Warden's Trail (4.6 mi. from trailhead at parking area on Stratton Brook Pond Road). This trail intersects the A.T. at Bigelow Col and provides the shortest route to Avery Peak from the south side of the range. Follow Stratton Brook Pond Road 0.4 mile east to Stratton Brook, the outlet of the pond, and another 0.4 mile east to a fork. Take the north fork (left) 0.3 mile to the old trailhead clearing. The trail bears northeast along an old tote road and ascends gradually 1.2 miles until the Horns Pond Trail diverges left. Climb more steeply toward Bigelow Col. The last 0.7 mile is very steep, rising 1,300 ft.

Horns Pond Trail (2.4 mi.) leaves the Fire Warden's Trail 2.3 miles from the first parking area on Stratton Brook Pond road. Climb gradually, first through hardwoods, then through a magnificent stand of spruce. Skirt a beaver pond at 1.3 miles. Climb gradually 1.1 miles to the junction with the A.T. Horns Pond is 0.2 mile north on the A.T.

Bigelow Range Trail (4.6 mi.) completes the traverse of the range westward from the A.T. near Cranberry Pond to Stratton

MAP

5

village. The blue-blazed trail (starting as a dirt road) leaves the Stratton Lumber Company road at its junction with Maine Highway 27, 0.6 mile south of the center of Stratton. Cross a brook at 1.0 mile (last water), and at 1.5 miles reach Arnold's Well (no water); at 1.6 miles reach top of ledges (good views); at 1.8 miles pass short side trail to "the cave"; at 2.9 miles reach summit of Cranberry Peak (elev. 3,213 ft.); at 4.0 miles reach Cranberry Pond; and at 4.6 miles reach the junction with the A.T.

Points of Interest

KENNEBEC RIVER Approximately 13,000 years ago, the ocean reached as far north as present day Wyman Dam, just upstream from Bingham, 420 feet above modern sea level. The land had been depressed by the weight of 4,000 vertical feet of ice which extended from Hudson's Bay to Cape Cod. As the climate warmed rapidly, the ice sheet melted and large icebergs calved into the sea as the retreating margin moved northward through the Kennebec valley.

Before the land rebounded, approximately 12,500 years ago, a large delta stretched into the sea. It can be seen today, high and dry at the northern end of the town of Bingham.

Other evidence of marine submergence includes the blue-gray silts and clays underneath Bingham. Periodically, perfectly preserved seashells, barnacles and seaweed, still smelling of salt water, can be seen in the river banks of the Kennebec. This geological evidence serves as a visible reminder that Maine went through rapid and dramatic climatic changes in the recent geologic past.

The Kennebec, one of the major rivers in Maine, has historically been an important transportation route. Maine's lumber industry used the Kennebec for many years as the most effective way to move enormous quantities of timber to market. The last log drive occurred in 1976. An interesting history of the entire upper Kennebec River area can be found in *The Kennebec Wilderness Awakens* by Mary R. Calvert.

THE ARNOLD TRAIL In 1775, General George Washington

MAP
5

appointed Colonel Benedict Arnold as commander of a detachment of 1,150 men. Their mission was to cross the Maine and Quebec wilderness and mount a surprise attack on Quebec City, a stronghold held by the British. In mid-September, the expedition left Cambridge, Massachusetts, headed north. The route followed across Maine was northward up the Kennebec River to "The Great Carrying Place," the portage between the Kennebec and the Dead River, several miles above present day Bingham. Here, they turned westward, following the old Carry Ponds portage trail used for many years by the native Abenakis to avoid rapids in the bend of the Dead River. They followed the North Branch of the Dead River until they crossed the height of land between the Chain of Ponds and the St. Lawrence River Basin near Lake Megantic in Canada. From this point they traveled north, following the Chaudière River to the St. Lawrence River and Quebec City.

Maine weather conditions could not have been worse. With their heavy wooden bateaux constructed of green wood, Arnold's dwindling forces spent nearly six weeks slogging through the swamps, rivers and bogs in this region of Maine. Reaching Canada in bitter winter-like November, Arnold's forces, reduced to 700 men, were unable to recover from their journey and stage a successful assault on the city. While the actual assault, which occurred in a blizzard on December 31, 1775, was a dismal failure, the audacity of the attack was enough to keep the British from fully exploiting the weakness of the colonists.

MAP 5

In 1935, CCC Forester James W. Sewall suggested a reopening of the original route of Arnold's march past the three Carry Ponds. This trail was known as the Arnold Trail route. The Appalachian Trail now follows about two miles of the Arnold Trail between Middle and West Carry Ponds. The Arnold Trail continues west for about three miles to Flagstaff Lake, which now inundates that part of the Dead River. The Arnold Expedition Historical Society maintains an active interest in the expedition and mounted a reenactment of the march in 1975.

Kenneth Roberts' novel, *Arundel,* provides an absorbing account of Arnold's ill-fated march to Quebec.

FLAGSTAFF LAKE In 1949, the Central Maine Power Company closed the gates on its newly constructed Long Falls Dam on the Dead River (west branch of the Kennebec River). A new lake began to form behind the dam's gates, transforming the Dead River valley from a series of farming communities along its meandering banks to a huge twenty-two mile long storage reservoir. The former villages of Dead River and Flagstaff now lie below the lake's waters. Occasionally, when the lake is drawn down, old bridge abutments, road beds, foundations and other signs of the old valley settlements emerge to provide proof that humans once lived, worked and died on the land that is now below the lake's waters. *Ghost Towns Of New England*, by Fessenden S. Blanchard, provides an interesting account of the displacement of the valley's inhabitants in 1949.

BIGELOW PRESERVE In June of 1976, a ten year battle between developers who wished to make Bigelow Mountain an "Aspen of the East" and an array of conservation groups led by the Friends of Bigelow, the Maine Appalachian Trail Club, The Natural Resources Council of Maine, and the Appalachian Mountain Club, came to a climax. A petition drive overrode a reluctant legislature forcing a referendum vote to create a 33,000 acre wilderness preserve protecting from development the entire 17 mile range and an appropriate buffer zone around the mountain's base.

The battle was bitter and divisive. However, on June 8, 1976, the citizens of Maine voted to establish the preserve by a narrow 3,000 vote margin. Thus, in one stroke, 17 miles of the A.T. was protected, as well as the entire mountain range, the finest between Mt. Washington and Katahdin. By 1987, almost all of the land had been acquired by the State through a combination of land swaps and purchases.

The Bigelow Preserve Management Plan calls for managing the Preserve "for a multiple of uses including wildlife, visual quality, recreational use and timber production." The overrid-

MAP

5

ing management consideration is "to maintain the overall natural characteristic and public uses of the Preserve as they existed in 1976 when the Bigelow Act was passed." The referendum clearly established that recreation in the Preserve require little permanent physical alteration of the environment and that users be dispersed rather than concentrated so as not to detract from the essential character of the natural surroundings. Much is owed to the individuals and groups who worked long and hard to "save" Bigelow.

During the relatively short hiking season, thousands of hikers hike all or parts of the range. To help educate users and to protect the resource, the MATC, in conjunction with the Bureau of Parks and Lands, supports a seasonal caretaker program at Horns Pond and at Bigelow Col.

MYRON H. AVERY When Judge Arthur Perkins became Chairman of the Appalachian Trail Conference in 1926, he enlisted the aid of Myron H. Avery, a junior member of his law firm. Myron Avery was a Maine native, a Bowdoin College graduate, who had gone on to law school at Harvard. Later that year, Mr. Avery moved to Washington, D.C., became one of the founding members of the Potomac Appalachian Trail Club, and was elected as its first president. For the next few years, Perkins and Avery worked closely together in all Trail activities from recruiting volunteers to flagging and constructing trail to writing manuals and guides until Mr. Perkins' death in 1932. Mr. Avery was elected Chairman of the Appalachian Trail Conference in 1931, a position he held until 1952. His leadership was instrumental in organizing clubs to carry through the entire Trail, and it was due to his leadership that it became a reality. By 1936, he became the first "2000 Miler" having walked and measured the entire Trail as part of the Trail building process.

He would not give up the plan of making Katahdin the northern terminus of the Trail. In 1935, he founded the Maine Appalachian Trail Club and was its Overseer of Trails until 1949, when he became its President. He held that office until his death in 1952. While many people have contributed to the

MAP
5

reality of the Trail in Maine, it was Mr. Avery in those early years who interested them in the project. He measured Maine's original 269 miles, wrote the Trail data, arranged for the CCC construction work (and later for the campsites), and each year did much personally toward the maintenance of this Trail.

Myron Avery believed in and epitomized the volunteer effort which is required to maintain the Trail. He developed the model followed today which combines individual volunteer efforts for maintaining the Trail with long-term federal protection of the Trailway helping to protect the uninterrupted character of the Trail from incompatible encroaching land uses.

The Myron H. Avery Memorial Lean-to was constructed to honor his part in the formation of the Trail. And, by an Act of the Maine Legislature, the East Peak of Bigelow, a range he loved, was designated as Myron H. Avery Peak.

References and Suggested Reading

Bigelow Preserve Management Plan, Maine State Department of Inland Fisheries and Wildlife, Department of Conservation, 1989.

Blanchard, Fessenden S., *Ghost Towns Of New England*, Dodd, Mead & Co., New York, NY, 1960, pp. 93–108.

Calvert, Mary R., *The Kennebec Wilderness Awakens*, Twin City Printery, Lewiston, ME, 1986, 584 pages.

Codman, John, *Arnold's Expedition To Quebec*, MacMillan Co., London, 1901, 340 pages.

Roberts, Kenneth, *March To Quebec: Journals Of The Members Of Arnold's Expedition*, Doubleday & Sons, Garden City, NY, 1940, 1947, 720 pages.

Roberts, Kenneth, *Arundel*, Doubleday & Sons, Garden City, NY, 1933, 486 pages. (also in paperback by Fawcett Book Co.).

MAP

5

MAP 6
Maine Highway 27 to Maine Highway 17

Location
Mountains of west central Maine, approximately 10 miles south and east of Rangeley.

Section Information
Section 8:   Maine Highway 27 to Maine Highway 4
Section 9:   Maine Highway 4 to Maine Highway 17

	Section 8	Section 9	Map Total
Length	32.2 mi.	13.1 mi.	45.3 mi.
Hiking Time	2–4 days	1 day	3–5 days
Elevation Gain			
Southbound	10,000 ft.	2,200 ft.	12,200 ft.
Northbound	09,600 ft.	1,600 ft.	11,200 ft.
Lean-tos & Campsites	4	2	6
Major Peaks	8 summits	None	
	North Crocker		(4,228 ft.)
	South Crocker		(4,010 ft.)
	Sugarloaf Mtn. (side tr.)		(4,237 ft.)
	Spaulding Mtn. (side tr.)		(3,988 ft.)
	Mt. Abraham (side tr.)		(4,043 ft.)
	Saddleback Junior		(3,655 ft.)
	The Horn		(4,041 ft.)
	Saddleback Mtn.		(4,120 ft.)

MAP

6

Trail Overview
The 32 miles of Section 8 are the most difficult along the A.T. in Maine. In this Section, significant gain and loss of elevation occurs as the A.T. crosses or comes close to six 4,000 foot peaks and crosses three other peaks above 3,000 feet. This is classic

mountain hiking featuring high peaks, deep valleys, open vistas, mountain ponds, and rock-strewn streams. The traverse above treeline on Saddleback Mountain provides a significant risk of exposure, particularly during inclement weather. Do not underestimate the time and effort needed to traverse this Section.

Section 8 begins at Highway 27 with the five mile climb to the wooded summit of North Crocker. South of the col, a short side trail leads to a rocky outcrop, the true summit of South Crocker. Descending steeply and crossing an old rock slide, the Trail passes Crocker Cirque Campsite. After a more gradual descent through a beautiful stand of large white birch, the Trail crosses the Caribou Valley Road and the South Branch of the Carrabassett River. Soon the Trail climbs out of a ravine to the high ridge between Sugarloaf and Spaulding Mountain and the junction of the Sugarloaf side trail. On a clear day, the half-mile side trip to the summit of Sugarloaf offers views that extend from Mount Washington to Katahdin. Continuing south, the A.T. follows along the densely wooded ridge and over a shoulder of Spaulding Mountain. Here, a bronze plaque commemorates the completion in 1937 of the final link of the Appalachian Trail. Beyond the short side trail to the wooded summit of Spaulding Mountain, the Trail descends to Spaulding Mountain Lean-to. The route continues along the ridge to the junction with the Mount Abraham side trail. This 1.7 mile side trail offers outstanding views in the last 0.5 mile along the open, rocky ridge of Mount Abraham. The sparsely wooded summit of Lone Mountain marks the beginning of the long descent to Orbeton Stream. Descending moderately and crossing Perham Stream, the Trail reaches Sluice Brook and the steep descent to the falls near Orbeton Stream. A moderate climb leads to Poplar Ridge Lean-to where the angle steepens before reaching the open summit of Saddleback Junior. To the south lie the open glacially-polished ridges of Saddleback and The Horn. For three miles, the open crest offers panoramic views. The steepening descent from Saddleback leads to Eddy Pond and a boggy traverse to Mud Pond and Ethel Pond. Piazza Rock is an interesting area to explore, with boulder

MAP

6

caves to the north, and the massive cantilevered rock which lends its name to the area. The Trail descends to the Sandy River at Maine Highway 4, the south end of Section 8.

Section 9 begins by climbing from the Sandy River valley to a watershed divide, passes South Pond and continues around a large boreal bog to the Little Swift River Pond Campsite. Beyond the highest point on the ridge, the Trail crosses a power line right of way, and descends to Sabbath Day Pond Lean-to, located in the heart of the Four Ponds area (Moxie, Long, Round and Sabbath Day Ponds). The traverse of Bates Ridge and Spruce Mountain completes Section 9 at Maine Highway 17.

Notable features of these sections include several of the 4,000 foot peaks in Maine: the Crockers, Sugarloaf, Mt. Abraham, and Saddleback Mountain.

Road Access

Maine Highway 27 crosses the A.T. at the northern end of Section 8, 5.2 miles south of the junction of Highways 16 and 27 in the village of Stratton or 18 miles north of the junction of Highways 16 and 27 in the town of Kingfield. Park on the old road on the west side of Highway 27.

Access to South Crocker or Sugarloaf Mountain: Caribou Valley Road is an unmarked gravel road leaving the south side of Maine Highway 27 about 1 mile northwest of the Sugarloaf USA ski area access road. At 4.3 miles from Highway 27, the Caribou Valley Road crosses the A.T. Although an important access for day hikers, the condition of the road varies considerably so it may not be possible to drive the entire 4.3 miles to the A.T. crossing.

MAP 6

Maine Highway 4, the division between Sections 8 and 9, crosses the A.T. 30 miles north of Farmington or 9 miles south of Rangeley. Park on the north side of the highway.

Maine Highway 17 at the south end of Section 9, crosses the A.T 26 miles north of Rumford or 11 miles south of Oquossoc. Park off Highway 17, 0.5 mile south of the A.T. crossing, not in the overlooks.

Supply Points, Accommodations, and Mail Drops

Stratton, population 700, is 5 miles north of the A.T. on Maine Highway 27. Stratton has restaurants, inns and motels, two grocery stores and a laundromat. There is a campground on the shore of Flagstaff Lake about 5 miles north of the village near Eustis.

Rangeley, population 1,400, is a popular year-round tourist resort located 9 miles north of the A.T. crossing of Maine Highway 4. Rangeley is a major resupply point. The Chamber of Commerce and an information bureau are located in the center of town. Services include: grocery stores, several restaurants, laundromats, banks, doctors, dentists, a pharmacy, hardware and outdoor sports stores, a repair shop and several hostels that cater to hikers. Rangeley Lake State Park, on the south shore of Rangeley Lake about 8 miles from the Trail, is a good site for day hikers staying in the area who wish to camp and swim.

Oquossoc, population 350, is 11 miles north of the A.T. crossing of Maine Highway 17, at the south end of Map 6. It has a small grocery, restaurants, and several camps and inns.

Rumford, a large town with all facilities, is 26 miles south of the A.T. on Maine Highway 17.

Post Office ZIP codes: Stratton, 04982; Rangeley, 04970; Oquossoc, 04964.

MAP
6

Side Trails

Sugarloaf Mountain Trail (0.6 mi.) Sugarloaf (elev. 4,237 ft.) is Maine's second highest mountain. Leave A.T. 2.3 miles south of the Caribou Valley Road and ascend steadily to the summit. Outstanding views make the 700 ft. climb very worthwhile. Several communication facilities and a terminal building for the gondola lift of the Sugarloaf ski area are located on the summit.

Mount Abraham Trail (1.7 mi.) The side trail to Mt. Abraham (elev. 4,043 ft.) leaves the A.T. 1.0 mile south of the Spaulding Mountain Lean-to. The last 0.5 mile of the trail is above treeline and offers excellent views of the surrounding peaks.

Points of Interest

LOGGING IN MAINE The view of the clearcuts at the head of Caribou Valley, as seen from the summit of Sugarloaf Mountain, clearly shows the changes in natural communities associated with extensive logging. Until 1840, farming was the principal occupation in Maine, with logging a close second. Since the turn of the century, the paper industry and timber management have surpassed farming. Tourism and year-round recreation are also important sources of income.

Historically, the logging industry passed through three stages: (1) the primitive, old pinewood times predating the Civil War, (2) the long logs (spruce) period from 1860 to 1890, and (3) the "pulpwood" phase in which four-foot lengths of spruce, fir and hardwoods were used in the pulp and paper mills. The latter stage developed at the turn of the century and continues today. There has been a recent resurgence of the spruce-fir lumber industry. The construction of biomass boilers used to generate electricity created additional local demand for wood and a market for wood slash as fuel. Much of the forests of Maine have seen four cutting cycles from the early 1700s to present.

The pinewood period was characterized by a very tough, difficult way of life for the logger. The pine trees were felled by ax, while teams of oxen dragged the huge logs to the streams. Logs were collected or "yarded" and then, during the spring run-off, were driven down the rivers to the lumber mills. Here the logs were sawn into boards with up and down saws. The hardships of men working in the woods and "driving" the logs down the rivers is well-documented. During this time, the rivers of central Maine flowing into the Penobscot played an important role in the development of Bangor. Bangor was a leading lumber producing town where 200,000,000 board feet of assorted lumber was produced during each year at the end of the period. During the Civil War period, the average yearly cut for the entire State was a billion board feet of lumber. In 1981, 2,629,000,000 board feet of round wood were cut in Maine for lumber, pulp, and specialty products.

MAP
6

With the resulting depletion of pine wood, the harvest shifted to spruce. Changes in this second stage were many including the development of steam sawmills with faster and sharper saws, the movement of loggers further into the wilderness, and the use of railroads and other mechanized equipment. Logging practices in the woods were essentially the same as in the early years.

Partly because of competition from western states, the scientific developments involving paper-making, and mechanized logging equipment, the end of the depression around 1880 found a revolution taking place in the Maine woods. This change was created by the shift to pulp and paper manufacture from the ordinary long-log lumbering operations. The pulp industry utilized logs of four-foot lengths which could easily be moved down the rivers and shipped to the mills by water or rail, and later by truck.

Methods of harvesting timber have changed dramatically. Today, mechanized harvesters are as important to timber harvesting as computers are to the office. There are eighteen paper mills and numerous lumber and specialty product mills in Maine. Landowners have developed a complex system of harvesting and transporting wood to the mills. As of 1976, the rivers of Maine which for centuries were used as vehicles of timber transportation, by law, could no longer be utilized for this purpose. Instead, wood is trucked or railed to the mill site. The result has been the construction of an elaborate system of gravel haul roads which frequently come close to or cross the Trail corridor.

A number of nationally known corporations play a key part in Maine's economy. These are Boise Cascade Corporation, Fraser Paper (which bought holdings from Diamond Occidental Corporation), Georgia-Pacific Corporation, Great Northern Paper Company, (now owned by Bowater Corporation), International Paper Company, James River Company, Lincoln Pulp & Paper Company, Madison Paper Industries, Champion International (formerly St. Regis Paper Company), and Scott Paper Company.

MAP
6

Today, Maine's 18 million acres of forest land cover 90 percent of the State's total land area. No other state is so heavily forested. More than 96 percent of Maine's commercial timberland is privately owned. The bulk of this land is managed to produce a wide variety of products. As commercial pressures in the market change, particularly the value of woodlands and lake shores for development instead of timber, the preservation of commercial forest resources in the state becomes more difficult.

SUGARLOAF MOUNTAIN   Sugarloaf is second in height only to Katahdin. The original A.T. route ascended the north slope of Sugarloaf (now occupied by the Sugarloaf USA ski area) and traversed the summit of the mountain. To avoid the development associated with the ski area, the A.T. was relocated in the early 1970s to its current route through the Caribou Valley, across the South Branch of the Carrabassett River, and over North and South Crocker Mountains. Today, the summit of Sugarloaf is reached by a 0.6 mile side trail from the A.T.

The open summit has several communications towers and buildings. On a clear day you can see from Mt. Washington in New Hampshire to the "end of the Trail" at Katahdin.

SANDY RIVER AND RANGELEY LAKES RAILROAD   See Canadian Pacific Railroad, page 112, for more information about the history of railroads in Maine.

SADDLEBACK MOUNTAIN   One of Maine's premier mountains, Saddleback is named for its saddle-like shape when viewed from the town of Rangeley. The extensive area above timberline offers delightful hiking with outstanding views in fair weather. Foul weather, however, with decreased temperature and visibility, coupled with the exposure to high winds, can be dangerous.

The wind-swept ridge is dominated by exposed bedrock on which scattered glacial erratics are perched. [Glacial erratics are rounded boulders left at random on the exposed bedrock as a glacier retreats.] Plant communities include sedge meadows, dwarf heaths, and krummholz. [Krummholz (i.e. crooked

MAP
6

wood) is the scrub forest of gnarled and twisted trees which form at treeline.] The area also includes a number of rare and unusual plants.

Saddleback supports some of the finest examples of balsam fir (*Abies balsamea*) and black spruce (*Picea mariana*) krummholz to be found anywhere in New England, as well as a rare example of eastern larch (*Larix laricina*) krummholz. These trees live at the edge of their range in a harsh environment of strong winds, high solar radiation, extreme temperatures, and poor nutrients. The twisted shapes of the plants result from many micro-climate inter-actions. Shelter from the prevailing wind creates an advantage, since wind blown snow crystals literally remove living tissues from the trees. Critical water loss occurs when cells are exposed to sun-light and warmed above the snowpack. In these marginal growing conditions any small gain or loss of advantage has a significant impact on survival.

PIAZZA ROCK Located on a short side trail immediately south of the stream crossing at Piazza Rock Lean-to, Piazza Rock is a flat-topped boulder cantilevered out from the cliff. This enormous rock supports a growth of mature trees. A short distance north of the shelter on the A.T. a side trail leads to an interesting series of boulder caves with many narrow passages.

BOREAL BOGS The extensive boreal bog about one mile north of Little Swift River Pond is an outstanding example of this distinctive type of wetland. A bog may look like a swamp or an open meadow with a small pond at the center, but it is very different. A bog often forms in a glacially-carved depres-sion where restricted water flow contributes to its develop-ment. Bogs are relatively common along much of the A.T. in Maine, particularly in the Mahoosuc Range. Unlike the more nutrient-rich marsh or swamp, the highly acidic bog literally preserves the organic matter accumulating on its surface. The floating mat of organic debris provides support for Sphagnum mosses and sedges which further expands the floating mat, eventually covering the surface of the water. Heath plants, like the waxy leafed leatherleaf provide additional support for the

MAP 6

accumulating vegetation. Most of the water in a bog remains out of sight below the vegetation. The growth of Sphagnum contributes to the acidity of the bog. This enhances the growth of "carnivorous" plant species like sundew and pitcher plants which are uniquely adapted to thrive in the nutrient-poor environment.

References and Suggested Reading

Smith, David C., *A History of Lumbering in Maine 1861–1960*, University of Maine Press, Orono, ME, 1972. 468 pages.

Wilkins, Austin H., *Ten Million Acres of Timber*, TBW Books, Woolwich, ME, 1978, 312 pages.

Wood, Richard G., *A History of Lumbering in Maine 1820–1861*, University of Maine Studies, No. 33, Second Series, 1935, 267 pp.

MAP
6

MAP 7
Maine Highway 17 to New Hampshire State Line

Location
Mountains of west central Maine, approximately 15 miles
northwest of Bethel.

Section Information
Section 10: Maine Highway 17 to South Arm Road
Section 11: South Arm Road to East B Hill Road
Section 12: East B Hill Road to Maine Highway 26
Section 13: Maine Highway 26 to New Hampshire state line.

	Sec 10	Sec 11	Sec 12	Sec 13	Map Total
Length	13.3 mi.	10.1 mi.	10.3 mi.	14.6 mi.	48.3 mi.
Hiking Time	1–2 days	1 day	1 day	2 days	5–6 days
Elevation Gain					
Southbound	3,000 ft.	3,500 ft.	3,300 ft.	8,000 ft.	17,800 ft.
Northbound	3,800 ft.	3,700 ft.	3,300 ft.	8,000 ft.	18,800 ft.
Lean-tos & Campsites	1	1	2	3	7

Major Peaks	Bemis Mtn. (3,592 ft.)
	Old Blue (3,600 ft.)

Moody Mtn.   (2,440 ft.)
Wyman Mtn. (2,945 ft.)

E Baldpate   (3,812 ft.)
W Baldpate   (3,662 ft.)

Old Speck   (4,180')
Mahoosuc Arm (3,765')
Fulling Mill   (3,395')
Goose Eye N   (3,675')
Goose Eye E   (3,794')
Mt.Carlo   (3,565')

MAP
7

Trail Overview

Leaving Maine Highway 17, the Trail descends into the valley of Bemis Stream and begins the climb of the Bemis Range. The five peaks (highest elev. 3,592 ft.) are partially open. Long stretches of connecting ledges afford views of the Rangeley chain of lakes to the north and most of the major peaks of western Maine. Bemis Mountain Lean-to is located near a spring between Second and Third peaks. After passing the Bemis Stream Trail which descends to Highway 17, the A.T. makes a high traverse on the east face of Elephant Mountain. The Trail reaches the col between Elephant Mountain and Old Blue Mountain in an area noted for its "old-growth" forest of red spruce trees. The A.T. continues over the scrub covered summit of Old Blue Mountain (elev. 3,600 ft.) offering outstanding views. The Trail descends from Old Blue through a fine hardwood forest to the top of the cliffs overlooking Black Brook Notch. From the overlook, the Trail drops 900 feet into the Notch, and crosses South Arm Road at the end of Section 10.

Section 11 traverses a rugged low mountain area with two spectacular notches rivaling Grafton Notch and Mahoosuc Notch to the south. Southbound, the A.T. climbs out of Black Brook Notch and traverses the wooded summit of Moody Mountain (approx. 2,430 ft.) where a spur trail leads to open ledges with a viewpoint into Sawyer Notch 1,100 ft. below. The Trail rounds the north edge of the cliffs and begins the steep descent into Sawyer Notch. The corresponding steep climb up Hall Mountain is visible across the notch. After crossing Sawyer Brook and a 4-wheel-drive road in the Notch, the 1,500 foot climb to Hall Mountain Lean-to is completed in only 1.4 miles. From the lean-to, the going becomes easier with a traverse of Wyman Mountain (approx. 2,945 ft.) and a more gradual descent to an old haul road at Surplus Pond. Following the traverse of several more knobs, the A.T. makes a gradual descent to the south end of Section 11 west of Andover at East B Hill Road.

Southbound, Section 12 starts on the East B Hill Road near Dunn Notch. The 60 foot high Dunn Falls and other cascades

MAP

7

on the West Branch of the Ellis River make Dunn Notch an area well worth exploring. From the notch, the A.T. climbs the long north ridge of Surplus Mountain, traverses high on its east slope, and descends to the Frye Notch Lean-to. From the lean-to, the southbound A.T. climbs gradually at first, then more steeply, climbing nearly 1,300 feet in less than 1 mile to the summit of the East Peak of Baldpate Mountain. Baldpate offers some of the best views of the mountain and lake country in western Maine. South of the traverse of the West Peak of Baldpate, the Trail descends past Baldpate Lean-to into Grafton Notch to Maine Highway 26. Grafton Notch State Park is a popular hiking destination with its own extensive trail system.

The Mahoosuc Range, a long chain of mountains straddling the Maine–New Hampshire border, offers classic mountain hiking, with some of the most difficult hiking anywhere on the A.T. There are nine major peaks, all over 3,500 feet, separated by rugged cols and notches. The total elevation climb in either direction is approximately 8,000 feet between Grafton Notch in Maine and the North Road near the Androscoggin River in New Hampshire. In the Maine section, the major peaks traversed from north to south include:

Old Speck (side trail)	elev. 4,180 feet
Mahoosuc Arm	elev. 3,765 feet
Fulling Mill Mtn., South Peak	elev. 3,395 feet
Goose Eye, North Peak	elev. 3,675 feet
Goose Eye, East Peak	elev. 3,794 feet
Goose Eye, West Peak (side trail)	elev. 3,854 feet
Mt. Carlo	elev. 3,565 feet

MAP
7

The numerous "low points" or sags between these peaks tend to be wet and boggy. The range is noted for its exceptional number of high altitude alpine bogs. In an effort to protect this delicate environment from trail impact, the Appalachian Mountain Club (AMC) has installed extensive walkways bridging the wetlands. Please stay on the walkways to prevent disturbance of these very delicate ecosystems.

Beginning at Grafton Notch, the A.T. follows the Mahoosuc Range Trail maintained by the Appalachian Mountain Club. The Mahoosucs are both a fragile and heavily used area, and the AMC maintains a caretaker at Speck Pond. A network of side trails provides access to the A.T. all along the range. Despite the boggy terrain, water may be difficult to find or reach along the ridge in periods of dry weather.

From Grafton Notch, the Trail ascends the north shoulder of Old Speck Mountain, with a side trail to the observation platform on the summit. Descending south from Old Speck, the Trail passes Speck Pond Shelter at Speck Pond, a fine mountain tarn, the highest pond in Maine. A traverse of the rounded summit of Mahoosuc Arm ends with a steep descent into Mahoosuc Notch, a deep cleft between Mahoosuc Arm and Fulling Mill Mountain. Giant boulders from the sheer walls have clogged the floor of the notch, resulting in a notorious stretch of Trail which involves clambering over, under, and around boulders for much of its one mile length. Snow or ice lasts well into June and can make passage difficult through some of the narrow openings. Extra time will be needed to negotiate this section of trail. From the west end of Mahoosuc Notch, the Trail climbs steeply up Fulling Mill Mountain. From the scrubby low-angled summit, the Trail descends to the col near Full Goose Shelter. Southbound, the Trail ascends two main peaks of Goose Eye, offering panoramic views of the Presidential Range to the south and the mountains of western Maine to the north. The ascent of Mt. Carlo marks the last peak in Maine before the Maine–New Hampshire state line is reached. From the state boundary it is another 16.7 miles to U.S. Route 2 in Shelburne, New Hampshire. The southern end of the Mahoosucs in New Hampshire is described in the *Guide to the A.T. in New Hampshire and Vermont*.

MAP
7

Notable features of these sections include: five major notches (Black Brook, Sawyer, Dunn, Grafton, and Mahoosuc); old-growth forest on Elephant Mountain; and the peaks of Old Blue, Baldpate, Old Speck and the Mahoosuc Range.

Road Access

Maine Highway 17, at the north end of Section 10, crosses the A.T. 26 miles north of Rumford or 11 miles south of Oquossoc. Park off Highway 17, 0.5 mile south of the A.T. crossing near Bemis Stream Trailhead. Please do not park at the overlooks.

South Arm Road, dividing Sections 10 and 11, leaves Maine Highway 120 just east of the Ellis River near the village of Andover. It crosses the A.T. about 7.7 miles north of Maine Highway 120.

East B Hill Road, dividing Sections 11 and 12, crosses the A.T. 8 miles west of the junction of Maine Highways 5 and 120 in Andover, or 6.5 miles east of Upton Village on Highway 26.

Maine Highway 26 in Grafton Notch State Park divides Sections 12 and 13. Bethel is 18 miles south on Routes 26 and 2. Upton Village is 8.5 miles north. Hiker parking is located on the west side of the highway about 0.1 mile south of the A.T. crossing.

These secondary roads provide A.T. access:

Sunday River Road provides access to the Wright Trail. This is the closest access in Maine to the south end of Section 13 at the Maine and New Hampshire state line. Sunday River Road leaves U.S. Route 2 about 3 miles north of Bethel. Follow the Sunday River Road west for 7.7 miles to a junction with twin bridges. Cross the bridges, turn right, and follow the dirt road (may be gated) 1.5 miles to the crossing of Goose Eye Brook. Trail parking is 200 yards ahead on the left.

Success Pond Road provides access to four side trails on the northwest side of the Mahoosuc Range. From NH 16 just south of Berlin, cross the Androscoggin River on the Cleveland Bridge, (Unity St.), keep left passing through traffic signals at 0.7 mile. The road bears right and at 0.8 mile crosses the railroad tracks and becomes Hutchins St. The road turns sharply left at 1.6 miles and passes the James River mill yard. Watch for trucks. At 1.9 miles from NH 16, the wide gravel road on the right is Success Pond Road. Take care in following the road as it is a major access for logging in the area. Trailheads are marked only by small Appalachian Mountain Club (AMC)

MAP
7

signs. From the north end, Success Pond Road leaves the west side of Maine Highway 26, 2.7 miles north of the A.T. crossing in Grafton Notch.

Supply Points, Accommodations, and Mail Drops

Oquossoc, population 350, is 11 miles north of the A.T. crossing of Maine Highway 17, at the north end of Map 7. It has a small grocery, laundromat, restaurants, and several camps and inns.

Andover, at the junction of Maine Highways 5 and 120, is 8.3 miles south of the A.T. crossing of South Arm Road. General stores, two bed and breakfast inns, and a campground are nearby. North of the crossing of South Arm Road is another campground located at South Arm on Richardson Lake. Andover is 8 miles southeast of the A.T. crossing of the East B Hill Road.

Bethel, 18 miles south of the Trail on Maine Highway 26, is a popular four season resort area. The town offers grocery stores, hardware stores, laundry facilities, bank, doctor, dentist, health clinic, pharmacy, veterinarian, and a selection of specialty shops.

Gorham, New Hampshire, at the southern end of the Mahoosuc Range offers a full range of hiker's services. Gorham is nearly 20 miles south of the state line where the trail description in the *Guide to the Appalachian Trail in Maine* ends. The services for Gorham are described in the *Guide to the A.T. in New Hampshire and Vermont*.

Post Office ZIP codes: Oquossoc, 04964; Bethel, 04217; Andover, 04216; Gorham, New Hampshire, 03581.

Side Trails

Bemis Stream Trail (6.1 mi.) The trailhead is 540 ft. south of the roadside parking on Maine Highway 17 (0.5 mile south of A.T. crossing). Reach the old railroad grade, 1.1 miles from the road, about 300 ft. south of the bridge over Bemis Stream. (This crossing is 1.0 mile south of the A.T. via railroad grade and provides a safe alternative when Bemis Stream is flooding the A.T.) The trail parallels Bemis Stream, crossing and re-crossing in the next 4 miles as it follows the Bemis valley west and

MAP
7

southwest and then leaves the stream and climbs to the ridge. Reach the A.T. 1.0 mile south of the West Peak of Bemis Mountain.

Cascade Trail (0.9 mi.) leaves the A.T. just south of the crossing on East B Hill Road and provides a 2.0 mile loop with the A.T. to the waterfalls of Dunn Notch (2.7 miles with side trails).

Table Rock Trail (1.5 mi.) Table Rock is the spectacular cliff that forms the northeast side of Grafton Notch. Leave the A.T. 0.1 mile north of Maine Highway 26 in Grafton Notch. Traverse and then climb steeply over boulders 1.0 mile to Table Rock, and continue 0.5 mile to rejoin the A.T. From the parking area the Table Rock/A.T. loop is 2.4 miles.

Eyebrow Trail (0.9 mi.) The Eyebrow is the cliff forming the west wall of Grafton Notch. The orange-blazed trail leaves the A.T. 0.1 mile south of Maine Highway 26 in Grafton Notch, reaches the top of the Eyebrow Cliff at 1.0 mile and rejoins the A.T. at 1.1 miles. From the parking area, the Eyebrow/A.T. loop is 2.3 miles.

East Spur and Link Trails (1.3 mi.) These form a difficult loop off the A.T. ascending the east spur of Old Speck. The route is not recommended in wet or freezing weather. The Link Trail (blue-blazed) leaves the A.T. 3.1 miles south of Maine Highway 26 in Grafton Notch and descends steeply 0.3 mile to the former site of the fire warden's cabin. Water is from the brook. The East Spur Trail leaves east from the cabin site and ascends steeply passing the Tri-boulder cave to the summit of Old Speck. From the summit, a side trail rejoins the A.T. in 0.3 mile at a point 3.5 miles south of the parking area in Grafton Notch.

Speck Pond Trail (3.6 mi.) Follow the Success Pond Road 12.3 miles from the Cleveland Bridge in Berlin, NH (or 7.2 miles S of Maine Highway 26) and turn northeast on a spur 0.8 miles to the trailhead. The trail follows the brook for 1.4 miles then climbs more steeply to the Joe May Cut-off Trail at 3.1 miles and reaches the A.T on the north side of Speck Pond.

Mahoosuc Notch Trail (1.9 mi.) Leave the Success Pond Road 10.8 miles from Hutchins Street in Berlin, NH (or 8.7

MAP
7

miles south of Maine Highway 26) to follow branch road northeast for 0.6 mile. Trail begins at a sign and climbs gradually to the west end of Mahoosuc Notch and ends at the A.T.

Wright Trail (4.0 mi.) This trail starts on a branch of the Sunday River Road. Follow the valley of Goose Eye Brook joining the A.T. 0.1 mile north of the East Peak of Goose Eye Mountain. The south fork of this trail leaves the A.T. 0.1 mile south of the East Peak and follows the prominent east ridge, rejoining the main trail in 2.5 miles, forming a loop.

Goose Eye Trail (3.0 mi.) Trailhead on Success Pond Road is 8.0 miles north of Hutchins Street in Berlin, NH (or 11.5 miles south of Maine Highway 26). Stay to the east (left) at a fork with the Carlo Col Trail. Cross two streams; pass the Maine–NH line at 1.4 miles and begin climbing more steeply. Traverse the main West Peak of Goose Eye at 2.9 miles and reach the A.T. in another 0.1 mile.

Carlo Col Trail (2.6 mi.) Use the same trailhead as the Goose Eye Trail. The Carlo Col Trail starts as a logging road and passes the Goose Eye Trail junction about 100 yards from the Success Pond Road. The trail follows old logging roads for 0.8 mile, crosses a brook and follows the valley for another 0.3 mile. Climb more steeply away from the brook and reach Carlo Col Shelter at 2.3 miles and the A.T. in another 0.3 mile.

Points of Interest

RUMFORD FALLS AND RANGELEY LAKES RAILROAD See Canadian Pacific Railroad, page 112, for more information about the history of railroads in Maine.

"OLD-GROWTH" FOREST   Natural, old-growth forest stands are rare in the eastern United States. To be considered "old-growth" by definition, a stand should contain a significant number of trees of long-lived species characteristic of a subclimax or climax forest. In addition, the area should appear nearly undisturbed by humans, with enough trees at least 100 years old to provide a distinguishable unit. At the col between Elephant Mountain and Old Blue Mountain an old-growth red spruce stand extends along the A.T. corridor for

MAP

7

nearly a half mile in each direction. The maximum life expectancy for red spruce is approximately 400 years. Some of the trees in this stand have been dated back to the 1620s.

NOTCHES OF WESTERN MAINE   Let us travel back 15,000 years to the time when the Laurentide Ice Sheet covered 2 million square kilometers of North America, from Baffin Bay west to Alaska, south to Montana, South Dakota, Ohio, and southeastward to New Jersey, Long Island, Cape Cod, and east to the continental slope on Georges and Browns Banks rimming the Gulf of Maine. From its central dome over Hudson's Bay where it reached a thickness of 4,000 meters (12,000 feet) of ice, it flowed radially outward and covered Katahdin, forming a vast, uninterrupted sea of ice. It looked much like the Greenland Ice Sheet does today. Although the northern latitudes of the Northern Hemisphere were once covered by ice sheets, only the Greenland Ice Sheet has survived.

Approximately 15,000 years ago, climatic warming started, forcing increased melting of the ice sheet. The highest mountains such as the Presidential Range emerged from the ice. As the ice sheet thinned, its far-reaching southern margin began to melt faster than ice flowing from Hudson's Bay could replace it, and it began retreating northward.

The margin had withdrawn to the present Maine coast by 14,000 years ago. New ice continually flowed from Hudson's Bay southeastward through the Appalachian Mountains while the ice arriving at the margin continually melted. The balance between supply from the north and loss (melting) was now tipped strongly in favor of loss. Continued thinning forced the ice sheet to flow into the lowest passes in the western mountains. Where previously it could flow over the mountains, the flow of fresh ice now squeezed through the narrow notches.

During this time, tremendous erosion of Grafton, Frye, Dunn, Sawyer, Black Brook, and Bemis Notches occurred. Melting ice produced running water on top of, in, and under the now rapidly melting ice sheet. In all the notches except Frye, evidence of the vast subglacial (at the bed of the ice

MAP

7

sheet) meltwater drainage systems abound (Thompson and Borns, 1985). The combined effects of pressurized water and sediment acted as liquid sandpaper, carving into the bedrock walls and floors of the passes. These drainage networks are seen in the eskers that snake their way through the western mountains, always searching for the topographically lowest points. When confronted by mountains such as Old Speck, the Baldpates, and the Bemis Range, the subglacial tunnels full of pressurized water and sediment were forced uphill, crossing through the western mountains at their lowest passes, the aforementioned notches.

Surficial geologic investigations in this area led by W. B. Thompson (1989) and others over the last several years have begun to unravel the style of deglaciation. For example, the floor elevation of Grafton Notch is 1,550 feet. The former subglacial drainage tunnel, now marked by a sinuous ridge of sand and gravel called an esker, climbs up to the pass from the north, indicating that the flowing water had to have originated in the ice sheet at an elevation of greater than 1,550 feet to have had enough hydraulic head to flow uphill and over the pass. These uphill climbing eskers can be seen winding their way from the north into the notches, giving us a picture of a rapidly melting ice sheet that was retreating to the northwest through the Appalachian Mountains.

The esker systems marking the former drainage systems of the ice sheet extend from near the present Maine coast, inland through the western mountains and down into the St. Lawrence drainage in Quebec. The esker running through Black Brook Notch is one of the longest in Maine and can be traced from Lewiston north to Andover, north through Black Brook Notch, and then beneath Lower Richardson Lake. Middle Dam has raised the lake level in Lower Richardson Lake and partly submerged the esker which is now seen as a series of islands (Leavitt and Perkins, 1935).

Between 13,000 and 12,000 years ago, the margin receded through the western mountains. For a time the retreat slowed

MAP

7

or halted and the ice sheet came to rest against the northwest flank of the Appalachians. Meltwater continued to pour off the ice sheet and was dammed in large glacial lakes by the Appalachians to the southeast and the still active ice sheet to the northwest. Glacial Lake Cambridge, named by Leavitt and Perkins (1935), filled the lowlands to the north of the Mahoosuc, Baldpate, and Bemis Ranges. The lake rose as high as 1,550 feet where it found an outlet, or spillway, through Grafton Notch. The large meltwater channel marking the former spillway is located to the west of Highway 26 in the floor of the notch. Vast quantities of meltwater spilled over the floor of the notch and thence down the Bear River carving many of the large potholes visible in the notch today.

Subsequently, the ice margin retreated again, allowing Glacial Lake Cambridge to now spill over across the floor of Dunn Notch at 1,450 feet. This outlet fed a much larger West Branch of the Ellis River. Again, northward recession allowed a new spillway to emerge and drain Glacial Lake Cambridge through Sawyer Notch at 1,450 feet. Finally, Glacial Lake Cambridge completely drained when the ice margin uncovered the Androscoggin Valley near Errol, New Hampshire. At this time, meltwater ceased spilling over the notches, the landscape became completely free of ice, and a shrub-herb-tundra vegetation was establishing itself on the bare soils of western Maine (Davis and Jacobson, Jr., 1985). The rapid establishment of vegetation stabilized the glacial landforms and preserved them in their final gasp, providing us the landscape we see today.

MAP
7

GRAFTON NOTCH STATE PARK Grafton Notch, a popular hiking center, is well known for its spectacular cliffs, outstanding waterfalls, and other natural features. The State Park, containing 3,132 acres, extends along both sides of Maine Highway 26 from the Newry–Grafton town line to about 1.5 miles north of the A.T. crossing. The Eyebrow, a cliff on the shoulder of Old Speck Mountain, forms the southwest side of the Notch. Table Rock, a shoulder of Baldpate Mountain, forms the north and east side of the Notch. An entire day could be spent exploring the waterfalls and boulder caves in the area including: Moose Cave (a narrow, deep flume, cool even on the hottest days); the Pools; Mother Walker Falls (complete with natural bridge); Screw Auger Falls (with potholes up to 25 feet deep); and the Jail (an enormous pothole). Immediately south of the Park, on land owned by the Nature Conservancy, is Step Falls, a series of cascades on Wight Brook with a total drop of 200 feet.

OLD SPECK Named for the speckled appearance caused by the mountain's exposed rock and its numerous trees, Old Speck marks the northern terminus of the Mahoosuc Range that stretches south to New Hampshire's Androscoggin River Valley. For many years, the peak was thought to be the second highest in Maine, until Sugarloaf was found to be higher. Old Speck commands one of the finest views of both Maine and New Hampshire from its summit fire tower, built in 1917. The now abandoned Fire Warden's Trail was considered by many to be the most uniformly steep mile on the A.T.

MAHOOSUC NOTCH Considered by some to be the "toughest mile on the A.T.," the notch is filled with huge boulders which have fallen from the surrounding cliffs. The Trail climbs over, around, and ducks under a few large rocks, where ice can often be found in mid-July. The spectacular sheer walls of Fulling Mill Mountain and Mahoosuc Mountain frame the notch.

HIGH BOGS OF THE MAHOOSUC RANGE The numerous bogs along the Mahoosuc Range are outstanding examples of subalpine bogs. The plant communities in these bogs are extremely fragile. They were formed in depressions along the Range and rely primarily on rainwater for moisture. The Appalachian Mountain Club has done an extensive amount of "bridging" work to help protect the area from hikers' feet.

A sphagnum moss (*Sphagnum fuscum*) tends to dominate the bog. It grows quickly, surrounding its neighbors, nearly burying them. These bogs often blow clear of snow and freeze to bedrock during the winter. The sphagnum moss is such a good insulator it will be very late in the season before the

MAP
7

frozen layers underneath will thaw. In some of the bogs, the peat may not completely thaw by fall. Perpetually cold soil makes it more difficult for other plants to gain a roothold in these high elevation bogs.

References and Suggested Reading

Davis, R.B., and Jacobson, G.G. Jr., "Late Glacial And Early Holo-cene Landscapes In Northern New England And Adjacent Areas Of Canada", *Quaternary Research*, v. 23, 1985, p.341–368.

Guide to the A.T. in New Hampshire and Vermont, Appalachian Trail Conference, Harpers Ferry, WV, 1992, 245 pages.

Hudson, Donald W., Jr., *Old Growth Forest And Subalpine Forest In The Mahoosucs, Baldpates, And The Bigelow Range*, Chewonki Foundation, 1987.

Leavitt, H.W., and Perkins, E.H., "A Survey Of Road Materials And Glacial Geology Of Maine, v.II", *Glacial Geology Of Maine*, Maine Technology Experiment Station, Bull. 30, Orono, ME, 1935, 232 pages.

Thompson, W.B., and Borns, H.W., Jr., *Surficial Geologic Map Of Maine*, Maine Geological Survey, Scale 1:500,000, 1985.

Thompson, W.B., and Fowler, B.K., "Deglaciation of the Upper Androscoggin River Valley and the Northeastern White Mountains, Maine and New Hampshire", *Studies in Maine Geology*, v.6, 1989, p.71–88.

MAP

7

Map Summary
APPALACHIAN TRAIL IN MAINE

	MAP 1	MAP 2	MAP 3	MAP 4	MAP 5	MAP 6	MAP 7	TOTAL
Length (miles)	40.8	43.3	30.4	37.0	36.3	45.3	48.3	281.4
Hiking Time (days)	4–5	3–4	2–3	3	3–4	3–5	5–6	23–30
Elevation Gain (ft) Southbound	2,200	4,800	5,900	4,200	8,400	12,200	17,800	55,500
Northbound	7,100	4,800	5,100	4,500	7,700	11,200	18,800	59,200
Lean-tos & Campsites	7	8	5	5	8	6	7	46
Major Peaks	1	4	5	2	4	8	12	36

7
Summary of Distances

Distances in miles
South *North*
bound *bound* **Lean-tos and Campsites—shown in Bold**

		MAP 1
0.0	**281.4**	Baxter Peak, Katahdin, northern terminus of Appalachian Trail
1.0	**280.4**	Thoreau Spring
4.0	**277.4**	Katahdin Stream Falls
5.2	**276.2**	**Katahdin Stream Campground**
7.6	**273.8**	**Daicey Pond Campground**
11.0	**270.4**	Pine Point
15.1	**266.3**	Abol Bridge (West Branch Penobscot River)
18.6	**262.8**	**Hurd Brook Lean-to**
21.1	**260.3**	Rainbow Ledges
24.6	**256.8**	Rainbow Mountain side trail
26.3	**255.1**	**Rainbow Spring Campsite**
28.1	**253.3**	Rainbow Lake Dam (west end)
30.1	**251.3**	**Rainbow Stream Lean-to**
32.5	**248.9**	Pollywog Stream (bridge)
33.9	**247.5**	Crescent Pond (west end)
36.3	**245.1**	Nesuntabunt Mountain
38.2	**243.2**	**Wadleigh Stream Lean-to**
40.8	**240.6**	Nahmakanta Lake (south end)
		MAP 2
44.0	**237.4**	**Nahmakanta Stream Campsite**
47.7	**233.7**	Pemadumcook Lake

156

SUMMARY OF DISTANCES

SUMMARY OF DISTANCES

104.1	**177.3**	**Wilson Valley Lean-to**
104.5	**176.9**	Canadian Pacific Railroad
104.8	**176.6**	Big Wilson Stream (ford)
107.9	**173.5**	Little Wilson Falls
110.7	**170.7**	North Pond (outlet)
111.5	**169.9**	**Leeman Brook Lean-to**
113.3	**168.1**	Bell Pond
114.5	**166.9**	Maine Highway 15

MAP 4

117.8	**163.6**	Side trail to Monson
120.8	**160.6**	Shirley-Blanchard Road
121.2	**160.2**	East Branch Piscataquis River (ford)
123.5	**157.9**	**Horseshoe Canyon Lean-to**
126.6	**154.8**	West Branch Piscataquis River (ford)
130.3	**151.1**	Bald Mountain Pond (outlet)
132.4	**149.0**	**Moxie Bald Lean-to**
134.5	**146.9**	Moxie Bald Mountain
136.5	**144.9**	**Bald Mountain Brook Lean-to**
136.7	**144.7**	**Bald Mountain Brook Campsite**
139.2	**142.2**	Baker Stream
144.2	**137.2**	Pleasant Pond Mountain
145.5	**135.9**	**Pleasant Pond Lean-to**
148.5	**132.9**	Holly Brook
151.2	**130.2**	U.S. Route 201

MAP 5

151.5	**129.9**	Kennebec River (ferry)
155.2	**126.2**	**Pierce Pond Lean-to**
156.7	**124.7**	Bates Ridge
159.4	**122.0**	Main Logging Road
161.1	**120.3**	East Carry Pond
162.6	**118.8**	Sandy Stream bridge, Middle Carry Pond Road
165.2	**116.2**	**West Carry Pond Lean-to**
167.0	**114.4**	Roundtop Mountain
168.7	**112.7**	Long Falls Dam Road

SUMMARY OF DISTANCES

171.1	**110.3**	East Flagstaff Road
172.5	**108.9**	**Little Bigelow Lean-to**
174.2	**107.2**	Little Bigelow Mountain
177.4	**104.0**	**Safford Notch Campsite** (side trail)
177.5	**103.9**	Safford Brook Trail
179.4	**102.0**	Avery Peak, Bigelow Mountain
179.8	**101.6**	**Myron H. Avery Memorial Lean-to** and Fire Warden's Trail
180.1	**101.3**	West Peak, Bigelow Mountain
182.2	**99.2**	South Horn
182.7	**98.7**	**Horns Pond Lean-tos**
182.9	**98.5**	Horns Pond Trail
184.6	**96.8**	Bigelow Range Trail
185.9	**95.5**	**Cranberry Stream Campsite**
187.0	**94.4**	Stratton Brook Pond Road

MAP 6

187.8	**93.6**	Maine Highway 27
193.0	**88.4**	North Peak, Crocker Mountain
194.0	**87.4**	South Peak, Crocker Mountain
195.1	**86.3**	**Crocker Cirque Campsite**
196.1	**85.3**	Caribou Valley Road
196.2	**85.2**	South Branch Carrabassett River (ford)
198.4	**83.0**	Sugarloaf Mountain Trail
200.5	**80.9**	Spaulding Mountain
201.3	**80.1**	**Spaulding Mountain Lean-to**
202.4	**79.0**	Mount Abraham Trail
204.6	**76.8**	Perham Stream
206.6	**74.8**	Orbeton Stream (ford)
209.3	**72.1**	**Poplar Ridge Lean-to**
210.7	**70.7**	Saddleback Junior
212.7	**68.7**	The Horn
214.3	**67.1**	Saddleback Mountain
218.2	**63.2**	**Piazza Rock Lean-to**
220.0	**61.4**	Maine Highway 4 (south of Rangeley)
222.1	**59.3**	South Pond

SUMMARY OF DISTANCES

224.8	**56.6**	**Little Swift River Pond Campsite**
229.4	**52.0**	**Sabbath Day Pond Lean-to**

MAP 7

233.1	**48.3**	Maine Highway 17
233.9	**47.5**	Bemis Stream (ford)
237.7	**43.7**	**Bemis Mountain Lean-to**
239.4	**42.0**	West Peak, Bemis Mountain
240.4	**41.0**	Bemis Stream Trail
242.1	**39.3**	Elephant Mountain/Old Blue col
243.6	**37.8**	Old Blue
246.4	**35.0**	South Arm Road
249.1	**32.3**	Sawyer Brook
250.5	**30.9**	**Hall Mountain Lean-to**
251.8	**29.6**	Wyman Mountain
254.7	**26.7**	Burroughs Brook
256.5	**24.9**	East B Hill Road
257.3	**24.1**	Dunn Notch
261.0	**20.4**	**Frye Notch Lean-to**
262.8	**18.6**	East Peak, Baldpate Mountain
263.7	**17.7**	West Peak, Baldpate Mountain
264.5	**16.9**	**Baldpate Lean-to**
266.8	**14.6**	Maine Highway 26
270.3	**11.1**	Old Speck Mountain (side trail)
271.4	**10.0**	**Speck Pond Shelter** and Speck Pond Trail
272.3	**9.1**	Mahoosuc Arm
275.0	**6.4**	Mahoosuc Notch and Mahoosuc Notch Trail
276.0	**5.4**	South Peak, Fulling Mill Mountain
276.5	**4.9**	**Full Goose Shelter**
277.5	**3.9**	North Peak, Goose Eye Mountain
278.7	**2.7**	East Peak, Goose Eye Mountain
280.9	**0.5**	**Carlo Col Shelter** and Carlo Col Trail
281.4	**0.0**	Maine–New Hampshire State Line

Index

INDEX

ACCIDENT REPORT FORM

Calm yourself and everyone else.

This form should be completed and carried out with anyone seeking medical assistance on the trail. It is presented as a public service by the Maine Appalachian Trail Club.

Day and Date: Time:

Accident Location:

Victim's Location:

What time did the accident occur?

Nature of the accident (fall, sickness, etc.)?

Describe injuries and their severity:
    What has been done for the victim?   When?

Victim's concise medical history:

Vital Signs:
    Time
    Pulse
    Respiration
    Pupil Size
    Complexion

What medication is/has the victim taken?
Check for medic alert tag.
Can the victim spend the night where (s)he is?
Can the victim walk out with assistance?
Will the victim need to be carried out?
How many people(capable of helping with a litter)
    are currently on the scene?
Victim's Name:
Telephone:

ACCIDENT REPORT FORM

Address:
Age: Weight: Sex: Height:
Group leader/Name: Telephone:
Address:
Group Affiliation:
Whom to notify, Name:
Telephone:
Address:
Other:
Plans of party attending the victim:
What special equipment will the rescue party need?

Before you leave the accident site to go for help:
• Note the victim's precise location on the map, circle it, double check it, and take the map with you.
• Coordinate and double check your plans with the party attending the victim.
• Leave at least one person with the victim and review the victim's condition before leaving.

Walk briskly (do not run) and take one person with you, if possible, to the nearest manned facility or to the nearest telephone.
• Convey the above information to rescue authorities, tell them the location you are calling from, and give the phone number.
• Await instructions from the rescue party.

Accidents should be reported to:

Maine State Police, Augusta, ME 04332, Tel. 1-800-482-0730

Appalachian Trail Conference, P.O. Box 807, Harpers Ferry, WV 25425-0807, Tel. (304) 535-6331

Maine Appalachian Trail Club, P.O. Box 283, Augusta, ME 04332

The format of this accident report form is similar to that used in the *AMC Guide to the White Mountains* and is used with the permission of the Appalachian Mountain Club, 5 Joy Street, Boston, MA 02108.

NOTES

NOTES